RAR Publishing, Oklahoma City, OK

ISBN 978-1-4507-2883-6

Cover art ("The Phoenix") by Teresa Moorhouse Howley. Used with permission.

"The Phoenix Cycle... an old part of us has to be let go and burn up for a new part to rise from the ashes."
www.teresahowley.com

See www.letterstosurvivors.com for more resources

Letters To Survivors:

Words of Comfort for Women Recovering from Rape

Compiled and Designed by Matt Atkinson

Foreword

There's something powerful about hearing words of hope from another person who's been where you are. A lot of people might offer encouragement and support, but when the words come from someone else who has lived through the trauma of rape, they have a depth of credibility. Try shouting "you don't understand!" at a woman who's been there, who's suffered through the same pain—it just can't be done.

Clinical therapists have all sorts of academic terms to describe the effects of rape—post-traumatic stress disorder, rape trauma syndrome—and each diagnosis comes with its formal list of symptoms. That's all well and good for coding medical records. But victims of rape are not collections of symptoms and problems, they are human beings struggling to repair their lives. There is one aspect of rape that can never be captured in statistics, and that is rape's power to make a person feel severed from the rest of life in a way that completely redefines loneliness. "I have never felt as alone as when I was raped," one woman told me. "It makes you feel like you've been ripped out of life itself." Another said "it makes you feel like you'll be a misfit forever."

In my work with victims of rape, I learned that all my clinical skill and education could only get us so far. I had become a specialist in several areas of counseling: sexual abuse, self-injury, eating disorders, domestic violence, and rape. I was good at it, too, but year after year I had a feeling that something was missing. Even as grateful patients discharged and returned to their lives, something felt incomplete. I learned that this was not just my own feeling; they felt it too. I had learned how to help rape victims work through nearly every symptom of rape trauma: flashbacks, depression, nightmares, panic attacks, sexuality issues, body issues, and more. During that phase of my life I worked with over 500 victims of rape, both men and women. All of these "treatment plan" details were resolved, and I was thanked for my help.

But something wasn't right.

What was missing was the sense of social community among Survivors. If rape's most toxic power is that it can sever the victim from her sense of connection to all life, then managing symptoms isn't the end of healing, it is merely the start of it. Healing from rape, by definition, means reconnecting the individual victim with a web of support. That's not just code for "support groups," either. It means something spiritually authentic and socially compassionate at once. Healing from rape *is* reconnection.

From that realization came my endeavor to form exactly that type of Survivor community. After writing the book *Resurrection After Rape*, women and men from around the world began to contact me to remark that it had helped them change their own lives. What they sought next was a group of "fellow Survivors" to share in that healing, to celebrate together. At first, this community gathered online at a forum I moderated. The group was carefully maintained to prevent its misuse, and the members began to trust and befriend one another.

In 2009, I created the first Spiritual Healing Retreat for Survivors, which attracted 18 women and offered an experience of camaraderie, disclosure, and humor in a serene wooded setting. Women overcame their fears to gather as Survivors, and in doing so began to also overcome their isolation. Each year, the number of women increased, and even included participants from other countries and continents. The pieces were coming together.

These endeavors allowed women who had formerly been isolated victims to connect with one another, building a scaffold of human spirits that collectively supported one another like the poles

6

of a tipi. The syndrome of alienation was beginning to heal. Since then I've heard something a hundred times that some people never hear in their entire lives: a room full of rape Survivors, laughing together in pure joy!

One friend of mine, Rachel, told me that she had spent years thinking of her rape as a time of loss, and she had listed all of those losses: self-esteem, safety, trust, health, happiness…But she said that a new realization had also come to her, that her rape had also given her all of us. Had she never been a victim of rape, she would never have sought a community of other Survivors to befriend, and would have missed out on some of the most rewarding relationships of her entire life. "I'm not minimizing my trauma," she said, "but I also need to be honest. In spite of all that I lost, I also gained all of you."

Whenever I ask my friends what they need most to help them heal, in every single case they give me the same answer: a social community of fellow Survivors. They make this absolutely clear to me. Healing has not come to them through clever therapies. Psychology has helped them manage their symptoms, but this must no longer be mistaken as "healing." Healing, they assert, comes from this near-tribal formation of a community in which each person is fully understood, appreciated, and invited. Such a phenomenon restores trust, humor, spirituality, friendship, accountability, loyalty, and self-respect, all of which are steps that defy the poison of rape. As Margaret Mead put it, the ideal culture is one in which there is room for every human gift.

"It was amazing to be with others who knew my story, and I didn't have to hide it or be ashamed of it," said 18-year-old Megan, whose letter is included in these pages. The very thing that conventional therapies prohibit is the medicine that most offers healing: friendship. Friendship is not a support group. It is not a scheduled gathering of victims who take turns hashing out their pain until it's time to adjourn for the week. Friendship is what happens when you are voluntarily accepted, where the loss of you would be grieved, where a missing person would be sought after, and where each person can say to the other, "You too? I thought *I* was the only one!"

When I asked for letters to be written to fellow Survivors, my friends jumped at the chance. I received letters from around the world. Some envelopes arrived with hand-drawn doodles to decorate them. Others had stickers that made bold statements—"Fight Violence and AIDS in Africa!" or the feminist "We Can Do It!" iconic poster—showing such a diversity of contributors. Letters were written from women ages 18 to 63. Some had experienced a single rape, some had been gang raped, some had endured years of abuse since childhood. All of them, every single one of them, approached this project feeling personally unworthy to contribute. Each of them worried that they weren't "healed" enough to deserve to say anything at all. Some worried they wouldn't know the right thing to say. Some worried they would sound trite. In every case, though, their anxiety was rooted in a common cause: they each respected *you*, the reader, and took you so seriously that they didn't want to offer you anything less than their very best.

What you are holding is a collection of the deepest pains and most amazing tales of recovery I have ever heard. Not one letter arrived from an anonymous writer; every single letter in this book was hand-written on paper by a woman I know personally. Jessica's letter arrived with tear stains still visible on the paper. She wanted to re-write it on "clean" paper, but I said no. "Your tears have made your letter clean...and holy."

I've chosen to reveal portions of the hand-written letters in the artwork of these pages so that you will connect with them. It is important to see that these are the works of women who are, right this very minute, living in this same world as you and spending each day trying to heal just a little bit more, too. I want you to see their writings, not just read them. See where they scribble out a word and try again as they struggle to reach you. See the hours and hours of effort they have made to tell you some honest things that come from their broken-yet-hopeful hearts, too. One letter-writer, Leitha, said of her contribution, "Of all the words I have ever written about my rape or the aftermath, these words—the words strictly devoted to others who have been hurt in like manner, hoping to help them sidestep even the tiniest pitfall—these are the proudest words I have *ever* written."

When a Survivor of rape utters words of hope and strength, they are not mere platitudes or slogans. Those words have been forged in a crucible of scorching turmoil. Those words, and the right to say them, have been *earned*.

This is not a book for people who want easy answers or a sweet pat on the back to make things okay. This book is for Survivors of rape who are in turmoil, who aren't sure there even is a way out of this, who struggle with the very question of whether to live or die. This is for the teen girl who hides the marks on her arms that she carves because she feels so alone. This is for the woman whose boyfriend has just called her "stupid" again. This is for the woman whose husband has lost patience with her pain because "you ought to be over it by now." This is for the woman in therapy for the fourth time, who is wondering if therapy hasn't worked because she's too messed up to heal. This is for the woman who knows that other rape victims exist, but has no idea if they're anything like her.

...I am writing this letter to le[t]
...now that I believe you, I support you
...understand many of the challenges that y[ou]
...facing, and I believe that you are no[t]
...you like me may have thought that yo[u]
...ost your strength, your trust, your wor[th]
...and at some times even your will to live
...please believe me that these attributes h[ave]
...temporarily silenced, not erased, whomever
...that fear is a great motivator never felt re[al]
...which is in fact incapacitating. I have s[uffered]
...both physical and emotional abuse at th[e hands of]
...a person who I thought I loved. The a[buse]
...eft me with feelings of profound humilia[tion]
...nd guilt and the belief that I did not dese[rve]
...o heal. Healing for me requires both forgiv[ing]
...myself and allowing myself to grieve. I hop[e]
...ome of what I have learned in the short [time]
...nce the assault will put you too on th[e road to]
...ecovery.

...Allowing myself to grieve for [my pain]
...nd hurt was one of the earliest and mo[st]
...teps. Like any trauma you will alway[s find]
...omeone who suffered worst than you. T[he]
...xtent and duration of other people's abuse c[annot]
...ffect your right to grieve for your own [pain]
...ill in time find that others who have su[ffered]
...vents similar to you and having allowed
...e space and time to grieve for are return[ing to]
...ormal happy lives. I want you to k[now]

I am writing this letter to let you know that I believe in you, I support you, I understand many of the challenges that you are facing, and I believe that you are not lost. You, like me, may have thought that you have lost your strength, your trust, your worthiness, and sometimes even your will to live, but please believe me, that these attributes have merely been temporarily silenced but not erased. Whoever wrote that fear is a great motivator never felt real fear, which in fact is incapacitating. I have suffered both physical and emotional abuse at the hands of a person that I thought I loved. The aftermath left me with feelings of profound humiliation and guilt and the belief that I did not deserve to heal. Healing, for me, requires both forgiving myself and allowing myself to grieve. I hope that some of what I have learned in the short thirteen months since my assault will put you too on the road to recovery.

Allowing myself to grieve for my loss and hurt was one of the earliest and most important steps. Like any trauma, you will always find someone who suffered worse than you. The extent, type, and duration of other people's abuse does not affect your right to grieve for your own loss. You will in time find that others have survived experiences similar to yours and have allowed themselves the space and time to grieve, and are returning to normal, thriving lives. I want you to now that it is ok to have a burning need to make others believe what has happened to you and to dismiss those who do not. Those who believe you will help you through the grieving process even when they don't know the right words to say, or when to say them. Please take comfort that they mean to support you and they represent the good you may be thinking has disappeared from the world.

There are no rules to follow from here on out but I want you to forgive yourself for the missteps we all make along the way. I want you to forgive yourself for having self destructive behaviors whether it be suicidal thoughts, like I've had, or alcohol and substance abuse like many other Survivors. Believe me when I write to you that the heightened awareness, shortness of breath, trouble sleeping, etc... will lesson with time and you will feel a desire to return to your normal activities. You will eventually need to tell others your story and along the way you will likely, accidentally, share it with someone you later wished you had not informed. Don't beat yourself up over their failures. How a person reacts is one hundred percent their responsibility and not yours.

You may have nighttime dreams that portray a life very different than the one you are actually living. Some dreams can be terrifying while others are fairytales of a perfect life. If like me, you wake up disoriented, do not feel guilty. It is only natural that our mind rejects the unthinkable, and so the unthinkable comes out through our dreams. Please understand as I do that healing is cyclical. You will have good days that will feel like the old you and bad days that can send you spiraling back into guilt and sadness. Please know that this is ok, this is normal, this is affirmation that you rise above (way above) the moral compass of your abusers. These emotions are an affirmation that what happened to you was wrong. Each of us has to confront self blaming beliefs. Did I send the wrong message? I should not have gone to that place. I should have fought or fought harder. But nothing we did made it ok for what they did. You were not hurt because you lost your power; you were hurt because someone misused their power. Any person that takes advantage of another deserves their own special place in Hell. (Yes it is okay to be angry.)

I hope that you will allow yourself whatever it is you need to heal. This is the time in which you are permitted to support yourself and be one hundred percent "you-centric." If you need space, take it. If you need time, take it. Seek out good therapy, journal to work through your own personal challenges, seek others in support groups. And please take pride in every one of your accomplishments no matter how small they seem. Twelve hours after I was assaulted, I presented my research at a national meeting. The man that assaulted me stood there and watched the entire time. Four days later, upon returning to my home town, I explained to a nurse that I was in the office for STD testing for the fourth time in front of a room full of happy expectant mothers. Six days after, I taught a class of forty-five students, two of whom also had a history of assault.

Please believe that this battle — and trust me, they do not exaggerate when they call this the fight for you life — will not be easy, but it will be worth it.

I can honestly tell you that the strong-willed, opinionated, good woman has returned and I will continue to fight because I am worth it AND SO ARE YOU!

— Love & Strength, Jill

I can honestly tell you that the strong willed, opinionated, good woman has returned. And I will continue to fight because I am worth it and so are you!

- Love and strength,
Jill

Elizabeth's letter is an example of the healing power of reaching out to others. In her letter she acknowledges feeling incomplete in her own healing, and yet she offers consolation to you, the reader. Elizabeth doesn't sugar-coat the healing process. Yet there is something very innocent, very childlike in her imagery: the yearning to cradle and sing to a wounded person is a very poignant, nurturing one.

We can tell a lot about a person's own needs by the things they wish they could offer to others, and in Elizabeth's letter we see words that reveal a wounded inner child. Perhaps this is a letter to any Survivor; perhaps it shows Elizabeth's love for her own emerging new self. Either way, writing this letter ignited a new sense of strength in her, and she closes with a realization that surprises her.

Dear Survivor,

I am so sorry that you must go through
what you are going through right now.
I wish I were there with you to hold
you. To tell _____ ll be okay.
To tell yo_ _____ urvive this.
Because yo_ _____ Survivor _____ have. You
are already a _____
I love you. _____ e love you.
I promise you, _____ e it through
this. You WILL mak_ _ through this.
I know it sucks. I _now it. I wish I
could say the perfect words. I wish I
could cradle you and sing away the
hurt, and confusion, a_ disgust, and
anger, and torment, an_ I am sorry that

Dear Survivor,

I am so sorry that you must go through what you are going through right now. I wish I were there with you to hold you, to tell you that you will be okay, to tell you that you will survive this. Because you will. You already have; you are already a Survivor.

I love you. So many people love you. I promise you, you can make it through this; you will make it through this. I know it sucks. I know it. I wish I could cradle you and sing away the hurt, confusion, disgust, anger, and torment, and I am sorry that I can't. I am in this boat with you.

The truth is, sometimes still I feel I am sinking. But I won't sink. This will not destroy me, or be the end of me. Neither will it be the end of you. I love you; you are a Survivor.

I wish that in this feverishly-scribbled note I could say some perfect thing, something that could undo what has been so cruelly done to you. I have faith in you. I respect and admire you. You are not alone.

I send this letter with more love and devotion than I even realized I possessed until this very moment.

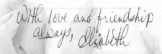

With love and friendship always, Elizabeth

Many of the women offered their personal words of advice to you. These were often my favorite parts of each letter, because advice often reflects the letter writer's personal truths. Wisdom can come from learning from mistakes, and a lot of women chose to confess their own in the hope that they can spare you the same fate. The most commonly-confessed mistake was "going it alone." Nearly half of the women write about their efforts to tough it out and heal without depending on anyone else, and every one of them admits they failed miserably.

If healing from rape means recon-necting with life, then a stoic effort to go it alone without anyone's help is self-defeating. Yet they each tried it anyway, and they each hope you won't do the same thing. I suspect that reaching out to you was done not only for your sake, but for theirs; over and over they told me that writing these letters had refreshed and inspired them as well. The most important thing in life is what the Ojibway Indians call *Gizhewaadiziwin*--"To love and care for others."

Hello—

My name is Amy, and although we
[me]t, I assume that we have rape i[n]
[h]onestly, the whole deal really sucks, and
[r]eally liked the ~~terms~~ terms victim and
[u]nderstand the important connotations [of]
[b]ut I don't want to be either. I didn'[t]
[see] myself (or anyone) and I still str[uggle]
some times.   Since I didn't turn out t[o]
Amy or Super Adventurer Amy (I really [hoped]
I have been giving a lot of thought to
I am not quite a victim anymore, but [not quite]
[up]on the horizon — I am somewhere in betw[een]

[It] isn't easy, you know that. But I can tell [you]
[it's] much harder to keep your secret. Kee[p]
[to] [your] body and soul. I still get

My name is Amy, and although we have never met I assume we have rape in common. Honestly, the whole deal really sucks, and I have never really liked the terms "Victim" and "Survivor." I understand the important connotations of the terms, but I don't want to be either. I didn't want this for myself (or anyone) and I still struggle with it sometimes. Since I didn't turn out to be Astronaut Amy or Super-Adventurer Amy (I really like those terms!), I have been giving a lot of thought to who I am. I am not quite a victim anymore, but "Survivor" is still on the horizon—I am somewhere in-between.

It isn't easy, you know that. But I can tell you one thing: it is much harder to keep your secret. Keeping it inside is toxic to your body and soul. I still get triggered sometimes and nightmares happen, but this is less often and less intense now. There have been some things I have learned along the way (and things I wish I knew then) that I would like to share with you. Maybe you'll find some of them useful.

1. Get into therapy. I tried and tried for a long time by myself, but this approach was no good. Don't wait until your thoughts are so dark and emotions feel out of control. The earlier you start, the better off you

... wanting acknowledged, that ... strong ...
handle myself. Now I realize ... simply
asking for and being open to help is a
strength and change. Therapy has ...
res, but to quote Bear Grylls (who I find
... nal & totally crush on), "I am really sear...
... res you have to commit." A last thought on
... find a therapist you connect with - as
... good credentials. My therapist's Kung-Fu
... he knows his stuff. More importantly, He ...
... orthy, warm and appropriately humorous
... ially, I have also noticed that he has ...
... way of inevitably being right & never ...
... n hook. :)

... stash of something funny around, stuff that
... aces you up. When you are having a bad
... days, or dark thoughts, it helps to give
... a break and create a mental change. I
... ourage, The Office & South Park (guilty pleasure)
... Bill Cosby on my cont...

will be long-term. I chickened out of therapy, of calling and asking for help, for a long time. I felt like seeing a therapist would be like admitting defeat, that I was not strong enough to handle myself. Now I realize that simply isn't true. Asking for and being open to help is a sign of strength and change. Therapy has been hard at times, but to quote Bear Grylls (who I find oddly inspirational and totally crush on!), "I am really scared, but sometimes you have to commit."

A last thought on therapy: find a therapist you connect with, as well as one with good credentials. My therapist's "kung-fu" is solid; he knows his stuff. More importantly, he is trustworthy, warm, and appropriately humorous. Incidentally, I have also noticed that he has this annoying way of inevitably being right and never letting me off the hook!

2. Keep a stash of something funny around, stuff that really cracks you up. When you are having a bad day (or days), or having dark thoughts, it helps to give yourself a break and create a mental change. I keep Entourage, the Office, and South Park (my guilty pleasure) on hand. At work, I keep Bill Cosby on my computer. His bit about giving his kids chocolate cake for breakfast is so funny! I've noticed that even a half hour helps me reframe, or maybe it is just a good old-fashioned distraction. Nevertheless, for me humor makes me feel human. It helps me open my range of emotions and just feel better.

figure out something creative about y___
___ it in you, I know it. Don't worry a___
___ing perfect or good @ it - it is the ___
___ the most important. I am not a gift___
___ I can't translate people & objects exactly as ___
But I still paint & draw & use colors ___
images. I consider myself an artist - an abs___
Ha-Ha. In my journal I draw a picture ___
of something that has impacted me that ___
use colored pencils, highlighters, markers, etc ___
I noticed my work was different the time ___
___ try to include another___ passive ___
some people write poetry, ___ Oth___
various crafts. It is just another outlet___
___ from yourself.

3. Figure out something creative about yourself. You have it in you, I know it. Don't worry about being perfect or good at it, it is the process that is most important. I am not a gifted artist; I can't translate people and objects exactly as they are. But I still paint and draw and use colors and shapes and images. I consider myself an artist, an abstract one! Ha ha! In my journal, I draw a picture each day of something that has impacted me that day. I use colored pencils, highlighters, markers, etc. Lately I've noticed my work was dark all the time, so I also try to include other more positive images. Some people write poetry, stories, or music. Others do various crafts. It is just another outlet to release your beliefs and emotions from yourself.

4. Eliminate violent and harmful music and media as much as possible from your daily life. I wish that I had done this much sooner when I figured out the impact it had on me. Shows [about violent crimes] kept me in a grey funk. It reaffirmed my belief that the world sucks and that people – men – are violent all the time. I feel hyper-sensitive to images of violence/rape against women. It's all over and suggested in movies, TV, etc. It is not subtle, either. When I examined my emotions after freaking out over an episode of Law And Order (by the way, I "examined" them like, 2 years later!), I realized that certain media keeps my world view dark and hopelessly cruel.

#3 lastly, "Be patient. It takes time"
therapist, Steve who has taken a lot [...]
healing Journey. I had no idea when I [...]
but it is like a mountian w/ peaks + vall[eys]
worried @ the beginning (+ some times still d[o])
3Not doing thurapy right. I get really hard [...]
unnecessarily. Not too long ago I contes[...]
that I fell off the therapeutic wagon—
old habits returned. I was nervous—[...]
I finally told him. He gently remind[...]
fall down seven times, we get up e[...]

Peace + Love,

—Amy

28

On a side note, I feel bad at lots of commercials too: perfect people, beautiful people in perfect lives…But that is a whole other thing, I guess.

   5. Lastly, "be patient, it takes time." I dedicate this to my therapist, who has taken a lot of time with me on this healing journey. I had no idea when I started this process, but it is like a mountain with peaks and valleys. I always worried at the beginning (and sometimes still do) that I am not doing it right. I get really unnecessarily hard on myself. Not too long ago I confessed to my therapist that I fell off the therapeutic wagon, that some of my old habits had returned. I was nervous and embarrassed, but I finally told him. He gently reminded me, "Even if we fall down seven times, we get up eight!"

Peace and love,
Amy.

Devin's letter reflects her personality. I know her to be a thoughtful, brave person, yet also prone to playing pranks, cracking jokes, and having the notion of "creative maladjustment" figured out. Her letter emphasizes the importance of using many emotions to heal. For Devin, recovery from rape cannot be stereotyped as turmoil and angst; she faces these, yes, but also remembers to include moments of laughter and wit.

One thing I particularly like about her letter is that it refuses to let recovery be corny or a sentimental positive-thinking superficiality; this letter urges you to let yourself feel all of what you feel. Tears, rage, sarcasm, humor—all of these are found in the process of healing. Devin's contribution to the tribe of Survivors is the reminder that a Survivor is one who accepts the full range of emotions that come with healing your wounds.

a hug with a pen and paper. If you were in front of me now, I'd just look you in the eyes. That eye contact would not be ackward, because gentleness in that exchange would speak volumes. Then I would hold you. Not in an effort to comfort, but because every tear that is shed is shared. Every shoulder shake would resonate through me, and when you choke on a sob, and my hug tightens, you will feel that I am feeling it too. When you were done, and your eyes were still puffy and red, I'd take you to have fun. Then, you would laugh harder than you cried.

You cannot forget laughter. You will need it, you will crave it. When your laugh echoes with others, it will feel right. That sounds hard enough, right?

A letter to a fellow Survivor is hard to write. Not because it is too hard, or because there are too many emotions, but because it is really hard to give you a hug with a pen a paper. If you were in front of me now, I would just look you in the eyes. That eye contact would not be awkward, because gentleness in that exchange would speak volumes. Then I would hold you. Not in an effort to comfort, but because every tear that is shed is shared. Every shoulder shake would resonate through me, and when you choke on a sob, and my hug tightens, you will feel that I am feeling it too. When you were done, and your eyes were still puffy and red, I would take you to have fun. Then you would laugh harder than you cried.

You can not forget laughter. You will need it, you will crave it. When your laugh echoes with others, it will feel right. That sounds hard enough, right? Trying to reconnect with others can be difficult. You have to just be you and do the best you can. What I am not saying is to pretend like nothing happened. Whether you trauma was ten weeks ago, or ten plus years ago, doesn't really matter.

This is not something you can handle on your own. I really ask that you seek someone to talk to. I don't mean just a friend or mentor, but a professional that knows and expects certain things from you. A good therapist won't care if you rarely, if ever, make eye contact during a hard session.

Trying to reconnect with others can
be difficult. You have to just be
you and do the best you can. What
I am not saying is to pretend
nothing happened. Whether your
trauma was ten weeks ago, or
years ago, it doesn't really matter

This is not something you can handle
on your own. I really ask that
seek someone to talk to. I don't me
friend or mentor, but a profession
who knows and expects certain thing
from you. A good therapist will know
that you have memorized every spo
in the carpet, or that you are very
familiar with the texture pattern of

For example, my therapist knows that I have memorized every spot in the carpet and the weave pattern on the couch I sit on when I talk to him. I know exactly how much the corners turn up on his floor rug. I happen to have a therapist who is a smart-ass who says, "Yep! The clock is still there" after catching me glance that way, not so stealthily!

Those times are hard. Sometimes it feels like you would rather get a root canal… or cut. But you need to keep going. It is literally one foot in front of the other. How ever long those steps take doesn't matter. What does matter is your forward momentum. There will be times when you slip back. It might be alcohol, cutting, or it might be isolation. What you need to do at that point is let someone know: an email to a friend, a voicemail to your therapist, a conversation with God… these will help you be ok.

…I just took a break from writing. About three months' worth! I wrote the above on a plane home from a Survivors' weekend retreat. I had forgotten what I wrote. When I read it back just now, I was surprised it wasn't full of sunshine, glitter, and unicorns! I am so happy right now, because the community of women is amazing, and I have never felt more connected to other people – ever.

women are amazing and I've never felt more connected to another woman - ever.

I wondered why it wasn't all sunshin-y, but then I realized that even in the midst of my retreat "high", I then knew what it was about to be a survivor, realizing tough times are ahead and bottom line - you will over-come. You have to do the work. You have to get through the sleepless nights and even realize that when you cry about your experience - its not bad! CRY! CURSE! OMG - Just don't keep it in!! Wonderful people can support you. Just remember that always - You have to work the hardest. But I PROMISE those are the most rewarding times!

I wondered why it wasn't all sunshiny, but then I realized that even in the midst of my retreat "high," I then knew what it was to be a Survivor: realizing tough times are ahead, but the bottom line is that you will overcome! You have to do the work. You have to get through the sleepless nights. And even realize that when you cry about your experience, it's not bad! CRY! CURSE! OH MY GOD-JUST DON'T KEEP IT IN! Wonderful people can support you. Just always remember that you have to work the hardest. But I promise that those are the most rewarding times.

Forever Fellow Survivor, Devin

Dearest Survivor,

Perhaps you don't even feel like a survivor ye
but the fact that you're alive means ~~the~~ ~~that~~
the worst is over. I know the aftermath is rid
with chaos and horrible feelings so unbearable th
ften seems ~~that~~ they're on the verge of
ming you. I promise it won't be that way foreve
rst, there are moments of light, moments wh
memories are not fighting to get out. Event
e memories only make occasional appearances.
y reappear at a convenient time, but you ca
them. Find something else to focus on—
d under your feet, notice what you
ee in the environment around you, breat
n't forget to breathe. We all need to
or there won't be any survivor
on to the next group. As sa
nd something small to help you th
night, ~~until~~ sometimes the nights are
Maybe it's just distraction at first
into something creative later, The
reation unto itself, and is one
ictories we can have. I know tha
take more effort than we feel we
in all of us. Love is in

Dearest Survivor,

Perhaps you don't even feel like a Survivor yet, but the fact that you're alive means the worst is over. I know the aftermath is riddled with chaos and horrible feelings so unbearable that it often seems they're on the verge of consuming you. I promise it won't be that way forever. At first, there are moments of light, moments when the memories are not fighting to get out. Eventually those memories only make occasional appearances. They rarely reappear at a convenient time, but you can live through them. Find something else to focus on—feel the ground under your feet, notice what you can actually see in the environment around you. Breathe. Don't forget to breathe. We all need to keep breathing or there won't be any Survivors to pass on hope to the next group. As soon as you can, find something small to help you through each day (or night; sometimes the nights are more difficult). Maybe it's just distraction at first, but it can transform into something creative later. The act of living is creation unto itself, and is one of the greatest victories we can have. I know that living can take more effort than we feel we have, but life is in all of us. Love is in all of us. They did not steal the most precious pieces of you, those pieces are just hiding. Please try to show yourself the same compassion you'd show toward a fellow Survivor. You need it just as much as the rest of us do.

Your sister in spirit,
Martine

Some letters hit all the important themes: you matter, you are not at fault, don't try to handle this alone, the rest of us are here for you, don't give up. I like the point Debbie makes about "locked doors": just because something you try may not help at first, it doesn't mean you are incapable of being helped. Not every person is a good ally, and some people could prove to be unreliable after all. Debbie is striving to point out that these are not failures that reflect your worth.

Rachel's letter is for the Survivor who has struggled with mayhem, even when it's self-inflicted: cutting, sex, suicide, nightmares, and shame. From those dangerous places has come a woman of insight, loyalty, humor, and integrity. Perhaps that is why Rachel's letter offers no sympathy for people who criticize Survivors ("just get over it!"); she sees how hard it is to fight for something that other people take for granted. What Rachel strives to say to you, above all else, is not to discard any resource that can help you: don't be careless with your allies, your friends, your fellow Survivors, because you will need every speck of strength they can offer.

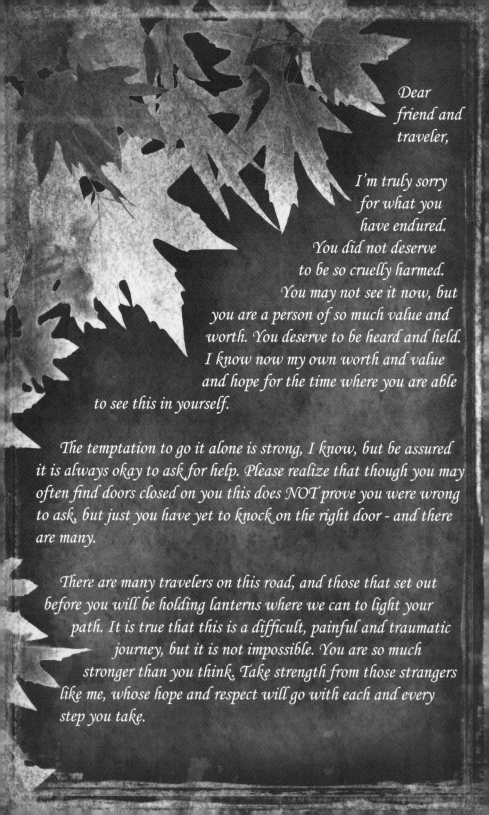

Dear friend and traveler,

I'm truly sorry for what you have endured. You did not deserve to be so cruelly harmed. You may not see it now, but you are a person of so much value and worth. You deserve to be heard and held. I know now my own worth and value and hope for the time where you are able to see this in yourself.

The temptation to go it alone is strong, I know, but be assured it is always okay to ask for help. Please realize that though you may often find doors closed on you this does NOT prove you were wrong to ask, but just you have yet to knock on the right door - and there are many.

There are many travelers on this road, and those that set out before you will be holding lanterns where we can to light your path. It is true that this is a difficult, painful and traumatic journey, but it is not impossible. You are so much stronger than you think. Take strength from those strangers like me, whose hope and respect will go with each and every step you take.

There may be times when you feel like you can't go on and you want to give up. It is okay to feel like this, rest a while and smell the flowers, but don't give up. It is worth it, you are worth it and you can do this. Sometimes the pain runs so deep within you seemingly with no end, remember it is right to cry and scream and shout and cry some more. Be angry, be sad, feel the depths of your feelings as from fear, anger, hatred and sadness comes peace, faith, compassion and joy.

I don't doubt you and hope and pray for the day where your doubts don't influence or shadow the person you can be. My thoughts are with you. I believe in you and with you everyday. Your friend and fellow rape Survivor.

Above all take it easy on yourself.

Debbie K.

Dear Beautiful Woman,

I know your world seems upside down right n[ow]
believe deep in your soul that you will not sur[vive]
even feel that living hurts too much. I will not [judge]
these thoughts or feelings; I have felt them too.
I am a survivor of childhood sexual abuse an[d]
I wish I had told someone sooner, and hope
trustworthy friend, a minister, a safe parent, a teach[er]
them what happened to you, and allow them to be [there for]
you to find more extensive help for you.

NEVER, NEVER be ashamed of yourself because o[f]
There is nothing you did wrong; don't ever let a[nyone say you]
"asked for it" or you "could have done som[ething."]
This has NOTHING to do with where you [were]
or what you were wearing. It is NOT [because of]
drinking, drunk or that your rapist was drir[king.]
No matter what.

Dear Beautiful Woman,

I know your world seems upside-down right now, and you truly believe deep in your soul that you will not survive this. You may even feel that living hurts too much. I will not deny you any of those thoughts or feelings, for I have felt them too. I am Survivor of childhood sexual abuse and of rape...yes, a Survivor.

I wish I had told someone sooner, and hope you will too. Find a trustworthy friend, a minister, a safe parent, a teacher, someone--and tell them what happened and allow them to be there for you and to find more extensive help for you.

Never, never be ashamed of yourself because of what happened to you! There is nothing you did wrong; don't ever let anyone tell you that you "asked for it" or "could have done something different." This has nothing to do with where you were, who you were with, or what you were wearing. It is not an excuse that you were drinking (or drunk), or that your rapist was drinking (or drunk). No matter what, no means no.

Please do not blame yourself if you did not scream or try to get away; you did what you had to do in order to save your life. Your spirit and love of life is not gone, it just feels like that some days. It feels very lonely sometimes. I know this, but you are not alone. Give yourself a little time to grieve, for a piece of yourself has been stolen so feel the loss. Find a group of women who have gone through the same ordeal as you, stay close to these women, because they can be strong, amazing allies and they can envelop you in love and strength.

There are those who will tell you to "get over [it]...
they are insignificant and don't deserve to be in...
do not have a right to tell you when you shoul[d]...
Take those people out of your life, they will h[...]
you don't need them!!

People will tell you that you will "get over it[...]
with you here, you will never get over it howev[er]
and anxiety will lessen. There will come a d[ay]
to smile again and see the sunshine. There [...]
when you are not constantly looking over your sho[ulder]
have panic attacks daily — or hourly, and the day[...]
smile for no particular reason and you feel safe [...]
safe again. You will reclaim your nights and[...]
when months and months will pass without a nigh[t]
[...] sleeping because you fear your nightm[ares]
[...]ll pass, I promise you. It may not feel[...]

There will be those who tell you to "get over it." Don't listen to them. They are insignificant and don't deserve to be in your life, and certainly do not have a right to tell you when you should be recovered from rape. Take those people out of your life. They will harm your recovery and you don't need them! People will tell you that you'll "get over it," but I'm going to be honest with you here: you will never "get over it."

However, with time the pain and anxiety will lessen. There will come a day when you are able to smile again and see the sunshine. There will come a time when you are not constantly looking over your shoulder, when you do not have panic attacks daily (or hourly). The day will be yours again when you smile for no particular reason and you feel safe again. You will feel safe again. You will reclaim your nights and there will be a time when months and months will pass without a nightmare. The anxiety you feel about sleeping because you fear your nightmares and reliving your rape will pass, I promise you. It may not feel like it now, but it will.

You may be struggling with your decision to go to the police and press charges against your rapist or not. This is a very personal choice. No one can tell you what you should or should not do. There are people, groups, coalitions, and agencies that will help you if you decide to go to the police. If you feel strong enough, take that help and stand up to your rapist, use that strength and fight. But please know that not every rape victim is in a position where doing that is an option, so don't feel you have to do it for anyone else. Your priority is you – taking care of you.

I hesitate to use the word "rape victim" to describe you, me, or any other woman going through this. You are a "woman wounded." As you know, wounds heal and so will you.

There will be days and maybe weeks when the sadness and depression is overwhelming. Don't get discouraged, it will get better. Never feel ashamed or allow anyone to call you weak if you need prescribed medications to help you deal with depression, anxiety, and sleep. It takes an extreme amount of strength to admit you need help, and then accept it.

I want to be honest with you about all of this, so there is something important I need to tell you. You may feel worthless because of what this man took from you. You may feel like you need to ignore or destroy those feelings by injuring yourself. This can happen in many ways. It may be that you cut yourself, or use alcohol, or become promiscuous. All of these are ways of injuring yourself and in the moment they may make you feel better. But afterward you will feel worse, and you continue in these actions because you aren't sure how else to get rid of the pain. Don't blame yourself, because these are common reactions. With the guidance and help of a therapist you can overcome these habits. Remember please that these things do not define who you are as a wonderful woman, they are a reaction to what happened to you.

I wish I could take these feelings and this pain away from you and protect you from them, but I cannot. This is your journey and you will get through it and come out stronger on the other side. Your spirit will be free once again, and you will see how beautiful and strong you can be. We may never meet, our paths may never cross, but please know this to be true: I pray for you, I love you, and I believe in you.

Love, Rachel

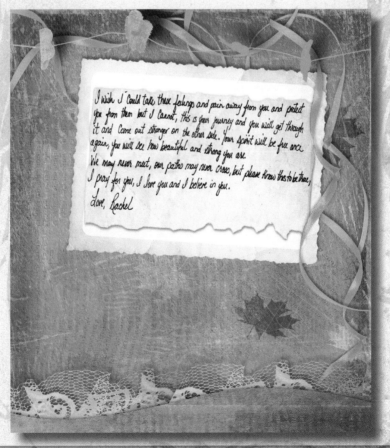

Megan is simply remarkable. She is eighteen years old, and had made the choice to face the pain of her rape directly rather than fleeing from it. I first met Megan at the Survivor's Spiritual Healing Retreat, which Megan had researched on her own before ever contacting me about attending. She had read my first book, begun to email me, and finally called me, all to get up the courage to board a plane and fly, alone, to a retreat where she would be among women she had never met. She was immediately accepted and loved by everyone, and we found her to be funny and brilliant. At times, Megan would cry –not in frustration or turmoil, but because (as she put it), "I'm so happy! I don't have to hide who I am, or feel ashamed of myself. I am so proud to be a Survivor!"

Her letter is crammed with wisdom.

Recovery is such an odd way to describe what we as survivors claim we go through. There ... of twelve step programs with chips and coins that you can look at to know you have reached your destination of being "recovered". There are no instruction manuals to meticulously follow but rather a map that has top spilled on it and ... rubbed out. The journey you are about to embark on is one that has no set features, and that is a good thing! This means that you have the power to personalize a recovery plan that works for you. Try different things, talk to different types of people that you trust, do beauty therapy...

Recovery is such an odd way to describe what we as Survivors of sexual abuse go through. There are no twelve-step programs with chips, no coins that you can look at to know you have reached your destination of being "recovered." There are no instruction manuals to meticulously follow, but rather a map that has pop spilled on it and parts rubbed out. The journey you are about to embark on is one that has no specific roles, and that is a good thing!

This means that you have the power to personalize a recovery plan that works for you. Try different things, talk to different types of people that you trust, do formal therapy, do unconventional types of therapy, but please know that something will work for you. It may take a couple of tries to find what kind of therapy works for you, but when you do find it, you will gain so much from it. Now, I am not saying it is going to be easy. It will be hard, and you will want to bang your head against the wall and give up. You'll have setbacks and triggers and things that seem too overwhelming to even think about, but you will get through it. And when you do overcome an obstacle, it is the most rewarding feeling in the world.

The first mistake that I made is letting other people define my own recovery. People may say things like, "aren't you over that yet?" or "you're still talking about that?" Do not listen to them, what they are saying may not be meant as harmful words,

People may say things like "Aren't you over that yet?" or "You're still talking about that?" Do not listen to them, what they are saying may not be meant as hurtful words but they are. No one can define or put a time line on your recovery. Not even you. Sometimes you will mark a day when you have done something great in recovery. You will be praised by your therapist, or by peers. And there will be more subtle realizations during your journey when you think back to a year ago and think "Hey, I have made progress." Being able to look back and see the improvements you have made will be more rewarding than anything anyone will say to you but they are. No one can define or put a timeline on your recovery, not even you. Sometimes you will know right when you have done something great in recovery. You will be praised by your therapist, or by peers. And there will be more subtle realizations during your journey when you think back to a year ago and think, "Hey, I have made progress." Being able to look back and see the improvements you have made will be more rewarding than anything anyone will say to you.

The other mistake I have made is telling myself the person I was before the rape is gone, lost, never coming back. I had myself convinced that there was not enough room in this world for the person I was before, and the person I was after. This is absolutely false. It will take time and effort, but with that you will see there is so much more to you than the trauma that has been inflicted upon you. The core characteristics that you were made up of before the abuse are still there. They may be covered up with things like anger and sadness at the moment, but I promise you they are still there. For me, the moment I realized my rapist had not taken everything from me was when I laughed so hard I cried, and then I started crying because I realized I was laughing again!

In the beginning I did not think I would get back to the point where I could laugh at silly things, but when I did it was the most victorious feeling in the world. For me, being able to laugh again was showing

and men experiencing someth
similar to what you are going
through. I have found the thing
...ch out about my ... ...e,
... people I find have
...ly ... something ...
... ... for you. ...
... just starting this
... you realize you are
... ...e, and among the sea
... people you come in contact
with, there is probably more th...
one person that can't relate ...
you and your story. There is on...
sentence I wish I would have hea...
in the beginning of my recove...
and there is I am proud of you
so I will say it to you. I am
proud of you for surviving. I
am proud of you for telling some
and I am proud of you for al...
the improvement that is so c...
—Megan Gardner

him that I would not allow him to take happiness away from me.

I know how hard recovering from something like this is. It is probably the hardest thing I have ever done, and I do not consider myself someone who is completely recovered. There are still things I need to work on and face. I just want you to know you are not alone, there are millions of women and men experiencing something similar to what you are going through. I found the more I speak out about my rape, the more people I find have been through something similar. My wish for you, a person just starting this journey, is that you would realize you are not alone, and among the sea of people you come in contact with, there is probably more than one person who can relate to you and your story. There is one sentence I wish I would have heard in the beginning of my recovery. And that is, "I am proud of you." So I will say it to you. I am proud of you for surviving. I am proud of you for telling someone, and I am proud of you for all the improvement that is to come.

-Megan Gardner

By far, the most common theme of these letters is "you're not alone." This is not a false platitude. It represents the core truth that these Survivors have come to realize, and the most precious thing they want to pass on. If rape's most potent effect is to make its victim feel isolated and unknowable, there is no more crucial salve than the message that you are not alone. Some of these women have survived suicide attempts, years of self-injury, addictions, abuse, and self-hatred, and yet they are the ones sharing their astonishing hope that Survivors are not alone!

For these women, with the combined centuries of pain they have endured, to unanimously produce the words "you are not alone" as their collective message to you, is a miracle. I can guarantee that it is a phrase every one of them would have disbelieved in their own lives in the not-too-distant past.

Hope came when they began to open up their truths and seek others who shared them. None felt eager to do this; it was a step that terrified every single one of them. But when they did, they found that other Survivors are an invisible "tribe" hidden in plain sight, just waiting for each other. I was astonished that every single letter I received contained some version of the words "you are not alone." It crystallized the truth that rape recovery is more than merely coping with clinical symptoms, but the development of social and spiritual bonds—friendships— among Survivors. "You are not alone" is the psalm of reconnection, the hymn that celebrates a way out of loneliness and back into connection with life.

I am sorry I have to write this for you. I feel so bad for you, for what you have endured. I too have endured a similar trauma. I want you to know that you are not alone, no matter how dark your days seem. I have to tell you how courageous you are, and how proud I am of what you have done. I kept silent for 16 years, I ran away from my emotions, from help, I put my feelings in a "box" and I tried to forget. Just recently I decided to get help. I have only shared my story with a few people. I have, like I said, just started my journey of healing and it made it that much harder by waiting so long. I give you so much credit for sharing your story, for standing up, and being so brave.

This is my second therapist. Don't be afraid to change until you find one that feels right. You need to be comfortable with yours, you will be sharing some private information, and you

I am sorry I have to write this for you. I feel so bad for you, for what you have endured. I too have endured a similar trauma. I want you to know that you are not alone, no matter how dark your days seem. I have to tell you how courageous you are, and how proud I am of what you have done.

I kept silent for 16 years. I ran away from my emotions, from help. I put my feelings in a box and I tried to forget. Just recently I decided to get help. I have only shared my story with a few people, and I've just started my own journey of healing and it made it that much harder by waiting so long. I give you so much credit for sharing your story, for standing up and for being so brave.

This is my second therapist. Don't be afraid to change until you find one that feels right. You need to be comfortable with yours because you will be sharing some private information and you need to know that you can trust them.

You also need to know that it is not your fault. No matter what, you could not change anything. You did what you needed to do to survive, and you did survive. During my rape I stopped fighting. My body and mind knew that this is what I needed to do. I am still coming to grips with this myself, but I know I did what was right. So did you.

Your body will heal. Your mind will heal as well. It just takes longer. Don't give up. Sometimes when I go outside at night I look at the stars. Some are brighter than others, some are big, some tiny. Some flicker. All of them are

Need to Know that you can trust them.

You also need to know it is Not
fault. No matter what you could not change
anything. You did what you needed to do to
survive And YOU DID SURVIVE! You did a
great job. During my rape I stopped fighting. My
my body + mind knew that this is what I
needed to do. I am still coming to grips with
this myself, but I know I did what
was Right - just Like you.

Your body will heal, your mind will
heal as well, it just takes longer. Don't give
up. Sometimes when I go outside at
night, I look at the stars. Some
are brighter than others, some are big,
some tiny. Some flicker. All of them are
surrounded by darkness.

surrounded by darkness. I often feel like a star. Sometimes I feel alone, surrounded by darkness. Sometimes I feel like one of the tiny stars, easily overlooked and taken for granted. Other times I feel like the brightest star in the sky, shining down as if to say, "Hey look at me! I am here! I am okay!" Even when I feel like that tiny star, I have to remember that if you take a step back and you look at the entire sky it is filled with stars. There will be days or even weeks that you will feel like that tiny star. Just remember that you are not alone. There are a lot of others who have gone through similar feelings.

We are all out here, together, all working toward the same thing: Recovery. It felt amazingly good when I realized that no longer did I have to hide. I found other women who understood, who knew, who "got it." When I tell my Survivor friends something they don't judge, they understand. There is comfort in that. Comfort in knowing that while each of our stories is different in details, we are all bonded by one thing and we understand what it means to have a bad day... or a string of them. There is comfort in knowing that when you think you are crazy they are there to say, "No, I understand totally."

If I could make a suggestion, it would be to find that group of fellow Survivors. Trust me — it makes a huge difference just knowing you aren't alone. I found my group online. For me it is easier to talk about my problems with others and not be face-to-face. You have to do what works for you.

Above All, don't give up. I will be the first to tell you - it hurts. All healing hurts. that is how you know things are healing - that they are going back into place.

Healing takes time and it isn't a race. You will be finished when you are ready.

I hope you find some comfort in these letters. Believe in yourself, and know you are never alone!

Karen.

Above all, don't give up. I will be the first to tell you, it hurts. All healing hurts. That is how you know things are healing, that they are going back into place. Healing takes time and it isn't a race. You will be finished when you are ready.

I hope you find some comfort in these letters. Believe in yourself, and know that you are never alone!

Karen

Dear Sister Survivor,

In my heart I am sad that you have had to find 'us', to join 'us', to read this book. We all know that these things should never happen, but the truth is they do, and we all in our own way have to live with the consequences — for our own lives and those of our friends and family. When I was brave enough to lift my hand up and admit that I had been raped, I was met by an amazing group of people who love, nurture and encourage me. When I was even braver and I could look them in the eye, my eyes filled with tears — tears of relief, joy, solidarity and understanding of an unspoken togetherness that they understood.

I don't know where you are in your journey, but even by reading this book and these letters, you are showing enormous courage. You have raised your hand, even just a little to say "yes, it happened to me too." This journey is tough, so tough. But you already know that, you are walking it. I hope that in reading this you will realise you are not alone in your journey.

Being raped was the loneliest thing I have ever experienced, possibly the loneliest thing anyone can ever experience. But the journey to resolution and healing does not need to be. It is hard to reach out, so very hard, but it is worth the slow, tentative, faltering steps it may take for you to do that.

There is no right book to read, meeting to go to, website to visit and you may stumble and fall as you try to find the right path for you on your journey. I would just implore you to never give up your quest. I often feel I stumble around with heavy snow boots on when flip flops would be so much easier to walk in. I truly believe those boots are labelled 'HOPE' and 'COURAGE'. Those are the things that have got me through the darkest of times and places. So, amazing Survivor, I will lend you my boots! I send them in my thoughts and really hope you can hold onto the fact you are walking daily with hope and courage – and that will get you through.

In my journey, I have really struggled with the harsh and horrible words spoken to me during my rape. I am now able to imagine myself being wrapped in a quilt – one that I have now made for myself. I call it 'the quilt of whispers'. It keeps me warm and safe and has embroidered in it words that I need to hear, and maybe words that you need to hear too. This is what I would say to you when you are struggling through those longest of nights:

"I want you to remember to breathe, to take small breaths and know that you will carrying on breathing, even though it may not feel like that. As you breathe, imagine a warm quilt surrounding you, shielding you from harsh and

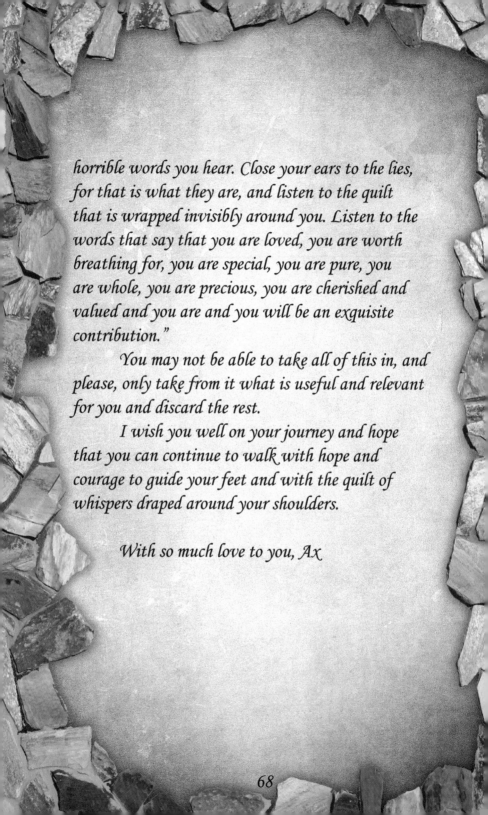

horrible words you hear. Close your ears to the lies, for that is what they are, and listen to the quilt that is wrapped invisibly around you. Listen to the words that say that you are loved, you are worth breathing for, you are special, you are pure, you are whole, you are precious, you are cherished and valued and you are and you will be an exquisite contribution."

You may not be able to take all of this in, and please, only take from it what is useful and relevant for you and discard the rest.

I wish you well on your journey and hope that you can continue to walk with hope and courage to guide your feet and with the quilt of whispers draped around your shoulders.

With so much love to you, Ax

This letter has been so long in the planning that now the deadline is here and I am still not sure what to say to you.

I guess in my heart I am sad, I am sad that you have had to find this, or is', read this book. We all know these things should never happen, but the truth is they do and we all, in our own way, have to live with the consequences for our lives + those of our friends and families. When I was brave enough to lift my hand up and admit that I had been raped, I was met by an amazing group of people who love, nurture and encourage me. When I was even braver and could look them in the eyes

Dear Fellow Survivor,

We have all survived, so we are all Survivors. I believe that we are at different places along that long, arduous path, but we can help one another along that path.

Many times I question whether or not I belong amongst other Survivors. As a wise person said to me, "trauma is trauma." Truly, our stories vary. However, we share sleepless nights, nightmares, body image issues, numbness, etc. We all share the effects of our traumas.

I was the person who entered therapy with anxiety and difficulty coping day-to-day because I hid the deep, dark secrets of my past from myself and still do at times…many times. I am that internally-fragmented person that you read about in books. I face a lost childhood that I cannot remember. My abusers are my parents. How could this be me? My world shattered in therapy. I felt alone, isolated, embarrassed, dirty, and crazy. Denial still rules my world a majority of the time. All I know is that I need to stay on this path because I owe something better to my kids, my husband, and myself.

This journey is the most difficult, scary, self-doubting endeavor that I have ever undertaken in my life. This journey has made me question, *Why me? Where was God? How could this have happened?*

We must persevere no matter how difficult this path is. I have found people along the path to help me: family, friends, fellow Survivors, and my therapist. Please find others to hold your hand along the path. Early on, my therapist said that it will get worse before it gets better, so please find those who can be there with you.

I felt so alone and isolated. I felt like there were no others like me. Then one day, I found the website "Pandora's Aquarium." I knew that I was not alone anymore. I could see myself reflected back at me in the words written by other Survivors. Many times, it would be phrased in ways that I would have used myself. Here at Pandora's, I found the "Resurrection After Rape" book and web community. Here was a more intimate community of Survivors working through their own traumas. I was no longer alone or isolated. In a world where I was made to feel unsafe, these sites have moderators and administrators to keep Survivors safe. These men and women in their journeys have become my heroes and inspire me.

Then I took a leap of faith and flew across the country to the "Survivor's Healing Retreat." I was frightened and terrified. I was afraid that I would not fit in. Once there, I instantly felt understood and that I understood them. I could see it in their eyes. These are some of the most beautiful people that I have ever met.

So please reach out to these communities of Survivors. Please join us. Take that risk. We will welcome you lovingly and we can take this journey together.

Exercise has helped me along this arduous path. Exercise is a way to help alleviate some of the stress that we face every day. Additionally, we can accomplish very positive outcomes with our mind, body and soul. Find the exercise that you like and start small.

Look for other resources like books, articles, and movies. Knowledge is empowerment. It has been helpful to read the science and psychology behind the trauma, as well as read other Survivors' journeys. Networking with other Survivors, exercise, and knowledge have put me in charge, whereas the assault and abuse took control away from me. Please take control of your journey in whatever way that means to you.

Angela Shelton, the filmmaker, has said the trauma of rape or sexual abuse is like walking around with a sword inside of you, clearly painful. Taking the sword out is also painful, like working through the trauma. The remaining wound hurts to heal, but as it heals the pain lessens. There will always be a scar.

We deserve to remove that sword. Join your community of fellow Survivors and we can help one another remove the sword.

Amy

Nearly every woman who wrote a letter talks about how difficult the healing process is. There are no shortcuts. Several of the women express a wish that they could take your pain in your behalf, saving you from it. They also say that they know this is not possible, and that you must make your own journey to face your pain and triumph over it. They know this because they have each done it. Hiding from the pain will not spare you from it. Pretending to be okay will not make you okay. Denying any connection between your rape and your depression, anxiety, or other problems won't work.

I asked the women to write honest letters, and they did. None of these letters is fluffy, charming positive-thinking sentiment. They tell the truth: healing from rape will be hard and painful. It will take a long time. It will test your very soul. You will only have the resources inside yourself to draw on that you work to put inside yourself, so if you waste your investment with things that don't matter you won't have inner strength to use. But if you fill yourself with things of depth, beauty, intelligence, wisdom, and honor, you will have all of these inner "medicines" when you need them.

The temptation to give up isn't rare. It's not just you who feels that way. These are amazing, strong, brilliant women...and every one of them had to wrestle with the same temptation to just quit.

What that would have meant—suicide? addiction?—is something we will thankfully never know, but I respect these letters for being absolutely truthful in addressing the pain and temptation to give up that you will feel.

I have never lost a former patient to suicide, but I have lost many to the trap of giving up. Some very precious people who had the potential to triumph chose instead to retreat, halting their journey and fleeing back into a world of constant distraction from pain, responsibility, and connection. Those are sad stories for me, because they lost and they know it. Yes, it is possible to fail. The women who wrote these letters are not going to con you by telling you everything will work out on its own. They will tell you the truth: that *whether* it works out, *whether* you heal, depends on you.

In the next three letters some important themes emerge. Tara's letter talks about the self-destructive shame that almost cost her life. Leitha's letter talks about the importance of making the choice to heal, not simply waiting for it to happen. Laura's letter addresses the common feelings of self-harm that many victims of rape later experience. But all three letters reach the same conclusion: the shame of rape belongs on the soul of the rapist, not on the Survivor.

Dear the bravest of the brave

Like every survivor who has attempted or who will attempt to write a letter to a future survivor I have agonized, truly agonized, over what to write and how to word what I felt in my heart. The trouble was I had no idea what I felt!

Who was I to be a source of inspiration to those in the most need? I felt so hypocritical. Here I was trying to inspire others with my words, my story, when I couldn't draw the same inspiration from it. I really wanted to say that the journey was worth it because the other side was, is, so amazing. But, I don't know that from personal experience.

I still self-destruct when the memories or therapy becomes too much. Just this week I took an overdose because I couldn't cope, couldn't deal anymore. Every day is a battle against the urge to self-harm. Every day is a fight against the urge to recall down the slippery and dangerous road of not meeting strangers for sex. Every day I must make a stand against the urge to binge, purge or starve myself of food just to feel a moments relief.

So why am I writing one? A dear friend once said to me that I remind her of a raft that is travelling down some rapids. I seem to disappear with the raft for a while, overwhelmed by the torrents of water. Then, as the waters calm and the raft upturns again; there I am, still aboard, still travelling downstream to the goal. This, THIS, is what recovery & healing is. Sometimes you are clinging to the raft like your life depends on it, sometimes you somehow manage to remain on board even after you have given up trying.

When I thought about this letter one thing I wanted to figure out what my message to survivors was. Once I got past my fear of not creating the perfect

Dear Bravest of the Brave,

Like every Survivor who has attempted or who will attempt to write a letter to you I have agonized, truly agonized, over what to write and how to word what I felt in my heart. The trouble was that I had no idea what I felt!

Who was I to be an inspiration to those in the most need? I felt so hypocritical. Here I was, trying to inspire others with my words, my story, when I couldn't draw the same inspiration from it. I really wanted to say that the journey was worth it because the other side is so, so amazing. But I don't know that from personal experience.

I still self-destruct when the memories (or therapy) becomes too much. Just this week I took an overdose because I couldn't cope, couldn't deal anymore. Every day is a battle against the urge to self-harm. Every day is a fight against the urge to freefall down the slippery and dangerous road of meeting strangers for sex. Every day I must make a stand against the urge to binge, purge, or starve myself of food just to feel a moment's relief.

So why am I writing one? A dear friend once said to me that I remind her of a raft that is traveling down some rapids. I seem to disappear with the raft for a while, overwhelmed by the torrents of water. Then, as the waters calm and the raft upturns again, there I am: still aboard, still traveling toward the goal. This, this, is what recovery and healing are. Sometimes you are clinging to the raft like your life depends on it, and sometimes you manage to remain on board even after you have given up trying.

When I thought about this letter, one thing I wanted to figure out was what my message to Survivors is. Once I got past my year of not creating the "perfect response," I thought about what I would have liked to have heard.

It's not your fault.

Okay, so I still struggle with this one too. So it definitely can't hurt to hear it over and over again. And it really isn't your fault. You cannot force someone to rape you. Period. If someone ever tells you that it was your fault, they are either totally ignorant of what rape actually is or they are not worth even one of your tears.

You are worth everything.

For a long time in my life I have felt beyond worth. One of the scariest moments in my life, outside of my abuse, was when I went to meet a man from the internet. I went, not because I really wanted to put a face to a person I had been conversing with, but because I really didn't care if he murdered me.

The last time I planned to meet a stranger I was beyond even that level of low. I knew this man was dangerous because he had disclosed dark fantasies and his job as a trucker made it fairly easy for him to dispose of me. And then one day I happened to be watching the news and a story came up about a young girl found murdered in the back of a car. I saw myself in this girl and I decided to cut all contact from that man. I haven't looked back since.

I had literally no self-worth for such a long time. I took so many risks with my life. Now it is more a battle of wills. The voice of strength is telling me that I am worthy, versus the voices of my abusers tell me I am not. Having our control and right to consent stolen from us can make us believe we were never worthy in the first place. This is so far from the truth that I am not sure I could ever emphasize it enough.

You are worthy, whoever you are and whatever they made you do. You are worth the world.

You are not bad because of how you coped in the aftermath. I ran for years from what happened (or

...sely-harming at around 13 years old, so I attempted to commit suicide for the first time at around 15 years old. Sadly, I have lost count of how many times I have attempted since then. I had an alcohol problem by the time I turned 16 so it fuelled my sexual (mis)behaviour; especially when I was using sex as a punishment myself.

I honestly didn't know why I was depressed. I was totally clueless to what I was enduring at the hands of a paedophile; unable to name it for years. I just thought I was totally messed up which added to the self-hate I felt. No-one could truly help me because they didn't know where to start looking. I was treated by some professionals (teachers, mental health workers) like a silly child. I often wondered if it was. Was my self-harm just a phase, something I should be growing out of? — The answer: No. Self-harm is an addiction not a teenage fad so it can happen at any age.

It was through beginning rape recovery that I learnt from other survivors that how I behaved was understandable, normal even. I hope reading this letter will help you begin to release the self-blame/hate cycle from your own self-destruction.

You may be told to, "just get over it", like rape is a fence you just need to hop over to reach the next field. When I hear this it makes me feel so invalidated so angry. And it is okay for you to feel this way too. Rape is huge. It isn't a scrape on the knee; it's a triple bypass, heart-stop surgery. No anaesthesia! It takes time to heal so er each person will heal at a different rate.

...thing I hate about being on this journey is that we have to ask the big ...stions, we have to go into battle & face our demons. I hate that. I wish I could ...hand that part off to my therapist - believe me; I have tried to more than once!

T...e about being on this journey is that we have to ask the big questions ... the great historical philosophers, the ones who won't be told by ~~reality~~ reality is. We search for the truth. We seek out the was still happening), most of the time not even realizing I was running away from something. In my early years I developed anorexic tendencies which morphed into bulimia during my teenage years. My teens were really when my self-destruction exploded. I began self-harming at 13 years old, and I attempted suicide for the first time at around 15. Sadly, I have lost count of many times I have attempted since then. I had an alcohol problem by the time I turned 16 and it fueled my sexual (mis)behavior, especially when I was using sex as punishment to myself.

I honestly didn't know why I was depressed. I was totally clueless to what I was enduring at the hands of a pedophile, unable to name it for years. I just thought I was totally messed up, which added to the self-hate I felt. I was treated by some professionals (teachers, mental health workers) like a silly child. I often wondered if I was. Was my self-harming just a phase, something I should be growing out of? The answer was no. Self-harm is an addiction at any age.

It was through beginning my rape recovery that I learned from other Survivors that how I behaved was actually understandable. I hope reading this letter will help you begin to release you from the self-blame/hate cycle that forms your own self-destruction.

You may be told to "just get over it," as if rape is a fence you just need to hop over to reach the next field. When I hear this it makes me feel so invalidated and angry! And it is okay if you feel that way too. Rape is huge. It isn't a scrape on the knee, it's a triple-bypass heart surgery with no anesthesia! It takes time to heal from, and each person will heal at a different rate.

The thing I hate about being on this journey is that we have to ask the big questions. We have to go into battle to face our demons. I hate that. I wish I could just hand that part off to my therapist...believe me, I have tried to more than once!

We are the warriors, the great historical philosophers, the ones who won't be told by someone else what reality is. We search for the truth. We seek out the pains of life and then we sheet them down. And we do so at our most vulnerable times. It is very easy to philosophize at times of peace, but to do this in a time of turmoil is a sign of our great strength.

My one bit of advice would be to never stop reaching out for support. Even if it takes every ounce of your remaining strength, never stop asking for help. We are all here for you. There will be moments when that is all you can do, but you will get through this. You are stronger than you could ever imagine. This is something I am learning along the way.

Sometimes when I want to give up because I am so sick of "healing," so sick and tired of working through my stuck points, I get so cross at my own strength. I want to yell at it, "why don't you just let me give up?!"

No one wants to be part of the "rape club," but something to help offset that is the wonderful community of Survivors out there. I have never met a group of individuals more compassionate and courageous than I have on this journey. No judgment, no exclusivity, no "proof of eligibility" needed. Everyone has value and is valued. They are who inspired my healing: we will not sink, we will not drown. We will swim together, my friend.

Take very gentle care of yourself, because you are so precious.

All my love,
Tara S.

I have been where you are. ...have
spent sleepless, terror-filled nights that
days. These will not
...meone who thinks they have won
...e they committed. But you knew
...e not beaten, we have not lost
...u find ...Dear Friend and Future Survivor,
...eugh ...You do not know me. You cannot pick
...ing I ...e make our journey through this life.
...rden, ... Somewhere in this world is someone who
...lie to ...gives little to no thought to the crime they co...
...insist ...And I knew. They are wrong! We are not bea...
...wave of ...though there will be full days you find it...
...ame - Kn... Spirit and hopeful, push through thos...
..., for the ...must not win. It is not an easy thing I ask...
...es ...I could release you from this burden, I m...
...Wh... feels too much, when "it" tries to lie to you...
...our control. look through your tears and insist...
...our control. Many times, there is blame - Kno...
...here shame to be shared among us, for the...
...not allow your mind to drift there, whe...
...t at fault. I was not. What binds us is...
...nd by living through the terror. In the...
...alone - realize your life ha...
...d a way to keep moving...

84

Dear Friend and Fellow Survivor,

You do not know me. You cannot pick me out of a crowd, or see "it" in my eyes, yet we are connected. What we share binds us as we make our journey through this life.

Somewhere in this world is someone who thinks they have won, or gives little thought to the crime they have committed. But you know. And I know. They are wrong! We are not beaten, we have not lost! Even though there will be full days when you find it impossible to remain full of spirit and hope, push through those dark days by insisting that they must not win. It is not an easy thing I ask of you—I know that. And if I could release you from this burden I most certainly would. When it feels too much, when "it" tries to lie to you and tell you there is no use, look through your tears and insist you know better. Prove you do.

At first, there is wave upon wave of emotion that seems out of your control. Many times there is blame, but know it is not yours. Nor is there shame to be shared among us, for that belongs to our attackers. Do not allow your mind to drift where shame resides. You were not at fault. I was not either. What binds us together is not a fault or fear. We are bound by living through the terror. In the darkest times, when you feel lost, small and alone, realize your life has value and purpose, and that each of us has to find a way to keep moving ahead. Keep living despite their attempts against us.

I have been where you are. I have lain where you lay. I have spent sleepless, terror-filled nights that drag into

...out wholeness m...

I waited a ... time for ... ...t.

...like the life I recognized. W...ing didn...

...stood still, hoping things would "get better", th...

I remained frozen. Don't make my mistakes.

...and healing—it rarely moves toward you. Find ...

with a caring and qualified therapist you trust

The path is rough and rocky sometimes, a...

But, there are many along the path to show you wh...

...not to stay. Listen to the counsel of go...

...soon as you are able.

...son of worth! There is value in

...reaching back to bring othe...

...many.

anxious, dread-laden days. These will not be forever. And feelings will return to you when the time is right. You will enjoy love and loving again. Be patient, and do not rush. You will know when the time is right to seek and enjoy those feelings.

My friend, in a wounded state it is easy to take the wrong path in your thoughts right now. Do not bring guilt, shame, bitterness, fear, or hopelessness on this journey. Those belong to the offender, not you. There is no room for these thoughts because we are on a journey to wholeness!

But wholeness may feel very far away from you. It did to me. I waited a long time for my life to return to normal, to feel like the life I remembered. Waiting didn't work. The longer I stood still hoping things would get better, the longer it was that I remained frozen. Don't make my mistakes. Move toward health and healing, because they rarely move toward you. Find competent help with a caring and qualified therapist you trust.

The path is rough and rocky sometimes, and much of it is uphill. But there are many people along the path who can show you where to step and where not to stay. Listen to the counsel of good and trusted friends as soon as you are able. You are a person of worth! There is value in surviving. And there is joy and thriving and reaching back to bring others along in this journey, too. There are many of us...too many.

There is an ability we all share, each of us in our own time, and in our own way: we have the ability and the need to trust. But trust is a learned behavior and can only

There is an ability we all share, each is our... ...way – we have the ability and the need to...

...earned behavior and can only be achieved by...

...someone with whom you can entrust your...

...be told.

There is no magic pill or potion to make this...

...Unfortunately, time does not "heal all wounds". But time...

...allows us to receive the necessary we need. Use the time wisely because...

...can feel real joy in your life again.

You may not recognize the exact moment it happens, but there...

...day out there, a day you must seek. The day you become a...

...survived.

...Love yourself, trust yourself, and move forward...

Reathe Brogan

be achieved by wise consideration. There is someone with whom you can entrust your story, and it needs to be told.

There is no magic pill or potion to make all of this go away. And unfortunately, time does not "heal all wounds." But time is a tool that allows us to access the recovery we need. Use your time wisely, knowing you can feel real joy in your life again.

You may not recognize the exact moment it happens, but there is a day out there, a day you must seek: the day you become a Survivor.

Love yourself. Trust yourself, and move forward.

Leitha Brogan

You are a daughter, a mother, a sister, a friend, a wife, and now you are a victim of rape. You have hit rock bottom, and although it may seem that there is no hope for brighter days, there is. If there is one thing that I wish I could make you do on your journey through healing, it would be to hold on to any ounce of hope that you can find. Right now you feel weighed down with the burden of a secret that feels like it has the potential to eat you from the inside out. I've been in your position. I have felt what you feel, and I've wanted to run from it as you want to run away. Run if you need to, but please don't run too far to find your way back.

There is someone who recognizes a change in you, and although they might not know what happened they wish you would open up to them. Find that person and confide in them. Draw strength from the spirit of all of us women who have fought the battle before you. I don't want to give you false hope or expectations that the journey to healing will be an easy one. It will be hard, terribly hard, and you will want to give up every day.

There will be days that you hate yourself and perhaps even try to hurt yourself. I have also had the desire to physically hurt myself for the actions of my attackers. Know that by doing this you are only adding to the issues that you will need to heal from eventually. It is a band-aid that will eventually need to be ripped from your skin and it will hurt much worse that if it were never there. Please realize that this is punishment that is misplaced. All the hatred, shame, and guilt that you feel belongs on the souls of your perpetrators, not yours. Don't think that the pain you are feeling is anything to be ashamed of. You have the RIGHT to be in pain, the RIGHT to be furious, and the RIGHT to seek justice for what you have suffered!

I think about you, and all of the women traveling this journey, every night. I pray that God gives you and all of us the strength to keep fighting, but more importantly, to keep loving. I pray that

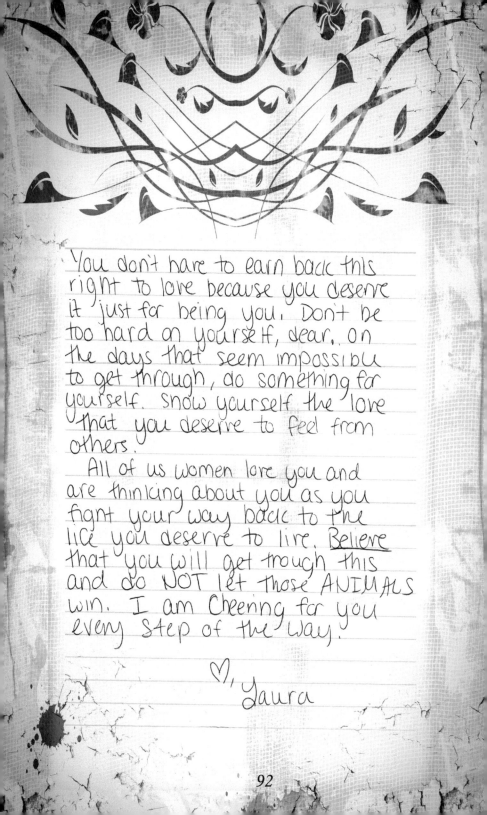

You don't have to earn back this right to love because you deserve it just for being you. Don't be too hard on yourself, dear, on the days that seem impossible to get through, do something for yourself. Show yourself the love that you deserve to feel from others.

All of us women love you and are thinking about you as you fight your way back to the life you deserve to live. Believe that you will get though this and do NOT let those ANIMALS win. I am Cheering for you every step of the way!

♡, Laura

you don't harden your heart from love that others want to show you, because you deserve it. You deserve to be loved and to give love freely.

    You don't have to earn back this right to love because you deserve it just for being you. Don't be too hard on yourself, dear. On the days that seem impossible to get through, do something for yourself. Show yourself the love that you deserve to feel from others.

    All of us women love you and are thinking about you as you fight your way back to the life you deserve to live. Believe that you will get through this and do NOT let those animals win. I am cheering for you every step of the way.

Love, Laura

I met Cassandra in a treatment center for adolescents several years ago. You can't miss her in a crowd: she has black and red hair, piercings, and wears T-shirts from vintage punk bands. She is also astoundingly creative, and maddeningly intelligent. Cassie devoured books of poetry and literature, and could play almost any musical instrument. We worked together intensely on issues ranging from sexual trauma, eating disorders, body dysmorphic disorder, and self-injury. She recently found me again to tell me, with pride, that she is completely sober, no longer harms herself, is in a happy relationship with a positive person, and has been free of depression and anxiety for years. After a full year without self-harm, suicidal thoughts, panic attacks, or depression, she celebrated her work by tattooing "SURVIVOR" across her upper back.

Second, please be aware
fail you at some point. By "car
about people who lecture and scol
crap. I'm talking about people wh
effort to love and nurture you.
can do is fit into the spaces o
real efforts to care. But at tim
A husband or boyfriend mig
details of your rape. Don't. It
details are to be shared in ce
a partner does not need to ha

A parent might overstep
comes to your privacy about you
treat you like someone who is
should be expected to work on y
continue your contributions to th
too. You are not too weak to be dep
to take for others; to help around
temptation to use trauma as yo
treat you like they think your rap
handle life, call them on it. Don
negative stereotype of rape victims

I have a therapist who is u
could work with a male therapi
others who were all women. I g
tried therapy with a male, and

96

Dear Sister Survivor,

I don't have a lot of soft and sweet words for you, and if you're anything like me you'll probably get sick of all the sentimental well-wishing you'll have to put up with from people who can never really understand. *"Oh, it will be okay"* or *"think positive!"* or *"look for the hidden blessings!"* That kind of stuff always makes me so angry, and I think it's because it shows me that some people really can't understand the pain my rape has caused.

I struggle with how to speak to you because my life has been a wreck and I don't think I'm qualified to be anyone's role model. So don't think of me that way, just because my letter's in a book.

First, and this may sound strange, do not hide from the word *"rape."* Don't make the word feel so powerful that you find yourself avoiding it, refusing to say it. Either you're dealing with it, or you're not…and I'm assuming that you're reading this because you want to deal with it. If it's something that makes you timid, it's something that's still got you submissive, not yet triumphant. The willingness to speak and write about our rapes is a sign we are no longer empty of power!

Second, please be aware that many caretakers will fail you at some point. By *"caretakers,"* I'm not talking about people who lecture you with that *"get over it!"* crap. I'm talking about people who actually make a genuine effort to love and nurture you. As humans, the best we can do is fit into the spaces of each others' lives, making real efforts to care. But at times we all make mistakes. A husband or boyfriend might demand that you share details of your rape. Don't. It will hurt both of you. The details are to be shared in confidence with a therapist; a partner does not need to have them to love you. I've never told my partner all of my details.

A parent might overstep their boundaries when it comes to your privacy about your rape. Parents should not treat you like someone who is fragile or helpless. You should be expected to work on your healing, but also to continue your contributions to the world in everyday efforts too. You are not too weak to be dependable, to keep your word, to take time for others, to help around the house. Do not give in to temptation to use trauma as your pass! And when other people treat you like they think your rape leaves you too delicate to handle life, call them on it. Don't let people continue the negative stereotype of rape victims as weaklings.

I have a therapist who is wonderful. I never thought I could work with a male therapist, but after trying several others who were all women, I got nowhere. I reluctantly tried therapy with a male, and it surprised me that it worked. My therapist is not perfect. He makes mistakes, says the wrong thing, lets me off the hook too easy sometimes and pushes me harder than I want to work other times. His jokes are corny. But he's kind. For all of his faults and flaws, the bottom line is just that: he is kind. Many times I've been pissed at him and considered just walking away, doing it on my own, telling him where he can shove it, and even attacking him by shouting that he hasn't ever helped me at all! But it's not true. I've had to re-learn my patience, and to give up my fantasy of ever finding a perfect caretaker. In the end, what I've needed most is loyalty and friendliness, not perfection. Don't idealize any therapist, but do be honest about needing one.

Avoid rape victims who are unhealthy. I mean spiritually or emotionally unhealthy, not physically ill. I know we're all supposed to talk like we're all powerful, wonderful women, but the fact is there are some real toxic people in our midst. Here are some warning signs of toxic victims to avoid:

• Someone who plays the "poor me, nobody understands me" game every time they get confronted (or pulls the whole "I knew you were a phony!" line anytime they are held accountable).

• Someone who uses their rape to entitle them to special care from others.

• Someone who constantly draws or writes things that are hopeless or preoccupied with horror, gruesome stuff, and pain. Honesty about pain is fine, but hopelessness is a warning sign.

• Someone who pledges to be a supporter, ally, or role-model, but then flees the scene when anything gets too real or uncomfortable. Beware of the "ally" who showboats about what a strong supporter she (or he) is, but who doesn't actually follow through when you need them.

• Someone who continually makes hidden threats against themselves—suicide, self-harm—to test your attention and loyalty.

• Someone who constantly proclaims they are trying to recover from rape, yet somehow you never see any meaningful attempts to change their lives. They still go on drinking, drugging, cutting, hating themselves, without sacrificing any of those habits for the sake of real growth.

I hope I'm not sounding too negative. I'm not a poetic writer like some of the other women. I just want you to be safe and heal. If you want to heal, you have to face your rape instead of hiding from it. It took me 11 years of alcoholism, drug use, cutting, and sexing before I was finally tired of being "messed up." During that time, friends who swore they'd be with me through it all turned tail and ran at the first sign of how hard this really would be. I wasn't sure it was possible to come back from that kind of pain. I was afraid I was too messed up to make it.

But [my therapist] never lost faith in me. At my lowest points, he believed in me. I thought he was a fool for having more faith in me than I deserved. At first, I wanted to heal just to honor him. But later I realized what he had been telling me the whole time: I can only heal for myself. What he taught me is what I want to pass on to you. Working to please a therapist, partner, family, or anyone else is the wrong motive. I am proud of myself. I never thought I could say that again, and for over a decade I couldn't.

I have not cut myself, taken a single drink, had any abusive relationships, or even hated at myself in mirrors for over four years now. I don't live to please everyone else. I don't eat, or starve, or have sex, or keep silent, to stuff my emotions. I also refuse to turn away when I see someone in pain. I just can't, not now that I know how it feels.

If you have just recently been raped, you don't have time to waste. You'll want so bad to ignore it, avoid it, convince everyone you're fine. You're not fine. None of us has ever been "fine" after being raped, and if you are "fine" after being raped, then you are clearly crazy! You'll fight it and fight it, and think nothing can ever put your pieces back together again. You'll feel disfigured, hateful, ruined for as many years as you try to stuff it rather than facing it, naming it, confronting it, and joining the rest of us Survivors with pride.

Please listen to the words of wisdom in this book. We are all telling you these things because we've been there. We're not phonies. We're not faking it anymore. We've all had to work through all sorts of hurt, blood, fear, shame, and wounds to be able to say these words. Today, we still have bad days, but we also laugh, play, love, pray, hope, and share. Please choose to be one of us.

Sincerely,
Cassie

While reading these letters, I noticed that not one of them tries to force any specific point of view on you, the reader. The writers of these letters had only one agenda: to support you, wherever and whoever you are, in your healing. There is no single technique; healing is as diverse in its forms as Survivors are in their spirits.

Given that rape is the ultimate crime of power and control, it is crucial that the support you receive from others not mimic coercion in any form. Finding no dogmatic pressure in a single one of these letters convinced me that the women who wrote them truly share a philosophy of healing. It does not matter what age or race you are, what spiritual path you are on, who you choose to love, what culture you are from, or how your rape happened; the predominant drive of each Survivor is to pass along the hope she's found to others who need it too.

I hope you will not merely read these letters and abandon this book to a bookshelf. If these letters make any impact at all, it will manifest in two ways. First, you will believe that there is hope for you if you choose to work for it. It will change your life, moving you to love and value yourself, your body, your soul, and your future. And second, you will feel motivated to share that hope with others in the future as well.

As the Ojibway people say, *Gakina Awiiya*--"We are all related."

Dear Sister,

I want to beg you not to give up on yourself, or on God, not on this world. There has been some pretty awful [stuff?] out there!

I'm not saying that rape exists [in?] made. I don't [believe?] God has ever [wanted?] anyone to suffer this kind of pain— God's will. [This was?] not God's punishment [it?] is not God's way of casting you off. [God?] is hurt with you, and is present in [what?] take to heal. I'm not asking you to have [sentimental?] feelings about God now. [Go?] then rage at God! Holler and accuse. Anyone who tries to pass off easy or simple religious formulas for healing [isn't taking you?] or God seriously.

I was [xx] sexually abused as a child of violent ways, and it left me with [dis?]figurements. Some of these are very [visible to?] onlookers, and some of them are things

Dear Sister,

I want to beg you not to give up. Not on yourself, not on God, not on trust, not on the world. There are even some pretty awesome guys out there!

I'm not sure why rape exists in a world God made. I don't think God has ever intended for anyone to suffer this kind of pain—this is not God's will. This was not God's punishment. This is not God's way of casting you off. I think God is hurt with you, and is present in the steps you take to heal. I'm not asking you to have gentle, sentimental feelings about God now…if you must, then rage at God! Holler and accuse and shriek! Anyone who tries to pass off easy answers and simple religious formulas for healing isn't taking you or God seriously.

I was sexually abused as a child in a lot of violent ways, and it left me with physical disfigurements. Some of these are very noticeable to onlookers, and some of them are things I can keep secret if I want to. It's been embarrassing to me when people make fun of my injuries, and it's almost as if people don't see the real me, just a bunch of disabilities. I struggle to find people who can see a human being beneath the "sexual abuse victim" layer.

What I want to say to you is that there is more to you and me than just a history of sexual abuse or rape. That is not who we are. Some people may have a hard time seeing more than that, but it's because they don't know how to look with their hearts. Your life must not be wasted in efforts to convince them, or force people to think a certain way, or constantly prove yourself to them. Your life must be spent becoming the kind of person you want to be. Be the person under the layers of abuse, don't be the layers of abuse.

When this happened to me, I was convinced I had been raped because I was an awful, wicked young woman. I thought I had rebelled in some unforgivable way, and that being raped proved what a fool I was. You might feel the same thing. I felt that it would be impossible to ever put my pieces back together. I was so broken inside that I thought my whole life would be a raped life. My whole body was a crime scene. I hated being a woman, hated what men thought about me, hated what I thought about myself. I attacked myself with my thoughts, and sometimes even with violence against my own body. I have never felt so lonely. I was just in college, and already my life had transformed from a future of potential to one of hell.

This is not some silly feel-good note where I say, "I don't feel like that anymore." I don't want to make this seem easier than it is, and make you feel lied to after you read this. But things have changed; things really do get better. There are still hard days, though. I didn't realize that each anniversary of my rape can be emotionally draining again: I get tense and I anger easily, I become numb, I have trouble making choices. What I've learned to do is start planning a week early before each anniversary, gathering friends to me, going on scenic trips, spending time in nature, and taking care of my body. This really does work.

Oh, and I do yoga now. Yoga has helped me begin to see my body as a living marvel, not a crime scene like I used to think. For a long time I couldn't stand to be inside my own body. I would disconnect from myself. Now I can feel amazed at the things my body can do, and I don't hate it anymore. My body is no longer my enemy. Find something physical to do, and befriend your body once more.

To get to this point, I've had to stop hiding from the fact that I am a Survivor of rape. I can say that out loud now! The very thought of that used to make me panic, but now I can actually say those words: "I am a Survivor of rape." The more I say it, the more power I gain. The word "Survivor" begins to eclipse the word "rape." I don't focus on rape, I just acknowledge it as part of my life's truths. I am many things, not merely a rape survivor. Remember that: rape does not become who you are. It merely becomes part of the fertilizer that produces your complexity as you grow. Many proud, amazing women have come through this experience; being a Survivor of rape is not a shame or a death sentence.

You will have to deal with critics. There are people who just don't get it. I was surprised how often my critics were women! In fact, the person I've met who most understands what I've been through is a man, so I don't think empathy is owned by just one gender. Neither is ignorance. Don't let other peoples' ignorance become traumas for you; have a thick skin, refuse to feel disgrace when you hear dumb comments, and just remember that there are also allies who do get it.

This is easier for me to write than to do. I have to face reminders of my abuse whenever I see a mirror. I almost become like the people who judge me, looking at myself and only seeing my past. We can't do that to ourselves. Recovery is not self-pity. Our strength is not found in our pain. Our strength is found in our hope. Never lift up your pain as the

thing I need to say: Do Not Commit Suicide
...e tried, or thought about it. I'm not sure
...istics are on that, but most of my survivors
...been through that mindset. Not very long
...s had to stay silent and alone. There wer...
...this, there were no survivors healing
internet forums, no support groups—
...only reason we have any of these today
men have begun to come forward and make
...ter than they were. Its still in progress,
...here are many ways things still need to
...se improvements will only happen if you,
...women our legacy, join what we're trying
...s make things continually better. If you
...de, all of us lose something. If you
...you are helping the world of rape victims
...if your life is a wreck, just being part of us
...lying out adds to what we're all doing. And
...nobody expects you to be perfect either. Just be
With Love, Jessica

thing you credit for your strength! Your pain is not what makes you stronger. Every time you refuse to repeat a bad habit, or challenge a self-defeating thought, turn away from a drink, go a little longer without cutting, or show patience with a person who is frustrating you, you become stronger.

One blunt thing I need to say: do not commit suicide. A lot of us have tried, or thought about it. I'm not sure what the statistics are on that, but most of my Survivor friends have been through that mindset. Not very long ago, rape victims had to stay silent and alone. There were no books like this, there were no Survivor's healing retreats, no internet forums, no support groups—nothing! The only reason we have any of these today is because people like us have begun to come forward and make things get better than they were. It's still in progress, though, and there are many ways things still need to improve. Those improvements will only happen if you, the next Survivor in our legacy, joins what we're trying to do and helps make things continually better. If you commit suicide, all of us lose something. If you struggle and persevere, you are helping the world of rape victims improve. Even if your life is a wreck, just being part of us instead of "checking out" adds to what we're all doing. None of us are perfect, and nobody expects you to be perfect either. Just be persistent.

With love,
Jessica

Dear Fellow Survivor,

When I was gang raped, people stood around and laughed at me the whole time. They cheered, they teased me, they acted like my worst pain was their party. I have never been so lonely as I was during that torture. People were everywhere, but all I felt was lonely, empty, and vacant. It's the most dreadful lonesomeness I have ever felt.

At the time, the guys who did that to me acted as if I was a toy for them. They thought it was hysterical, a wild time, a way to blow off steam on some stupid girl who didn't matter. They were wrong about every one of those things.

For years I had nightmares. I had panic attacks when I smelled liquor or heard the sounds of guys partying in movies. I thought I was doomed to a life of torment. I thought I had been damned to loneliness forever. I thought I was worthless, a loser, good for nothing but abuse. I was wrong about every one of those things.

I didn't have a dramatic story about breaking through my trauma. I worked my way back, bit by bit. I listened to a lot of music that promoted healing, and threw out all the music that degraded women (and I was surprised how much there was—including some by women musicians!) I

started to read feminist blogs and websites, and I learned that feminism is nothing like what I'd been told: feminists weren't bitter, humorless women with "man issues." They were smart, witty, fascinating people...and I wanted to be thought of that way, myself. Every time I heard someone on TV or the radio make fun of feminists as "man-haters" or "feminazis," I became so angry because they were insulting the one philosophy that was telling me I wasn't worthless! They were saying that women's concerns are silly, that women who want any value are nuisances. They were promoting the very mindset that my rapists had, and then laughing at us!

The hardest part of my shame for me is that I was a virgin when I was raped. I thought that being raped meant I had been defiled, and I was suicidal. What man would ever want me now? I had been ruined, body and soul. I also thought God would be angry with me because I had "had sex." I believed I had sinned. I even felt panic and nausea in any sexual situations I was in for years later. But I have learned some things since then that I want to share.

If you were a virgin when you were raped, you were still a virgin afterwards! Virginity is something that can only be given, not taken. Virginity is not about your body. It is about your spirit. Rape is not sex, and being raped is

not a victim's sin. I thought for a long time that I could never enjoy anything sexual because I always associated it with violence and horror, but those are not parts of sex. Once I learned that rape is not sex, I was gradually able to change my feelings of shame. We are spiritual beings, not just bodies, and our bodies do not define us. Fat, thin, White, Brown, old, young—these are ridiculous. They do not describe a human spirit. The term "rape victim" doesn't either. But "Survivor"? Oh yes—that describes a spirit.

As a rape Survivor, you share an experience that one in every four or five women also shares. It should not be the basis for our bonding together as women. It should not be a defining moment in our lives. It should not require us to come together. But it does, and we must. I have found a community of incredible, powerful women--and even men, too. And what we share turns out to be something far more worthy than a rape experience: we share a willingness to struggle together for a more just world. I've found strength in my willingness to take on this issue!

Take these steps as well. Start gathering your "healing music." Read literature by strong women, and by men who are pro-feminist. Remember that sex and sexism are not the same thing: enjoy one and fight the other! We know the same loneliness that you feel, and I was amazed to find that there are eons of prior Survivors who have helped blaze trails to healing. We don't have to figure out every step on our own, unless we turn down the opportunity to join a proud movement of Survivors.

-Mary

My dearest sister,

You do not know me and I do not know you but we are sisters. We are sisters due to the fact that we share the same pain from acts done to us by someone uncaring of our wants, needs, cares, or desires. Please let me show you a few ways that may help you to begin healing, or maybe help you on your recovery path.

First, recovery is different for each of us. No two persons' healing and recovery are the same. We are each unique, there so must our healing be.

As I am writing you this letter I am sitting outside enjoying the rain and accepting another day. To me, acceptance was just my first step. I had to accept that I was a victim, and that was the hardest part for me. I always thought of a victim as someone else laying down, crying, whining "poor me." That is not true! A victim is someone who is not allowed to make choices. Someone else selfishly decides what they want from you, and that is it. You can beg, you can cry, you can scream and fight, but you must accept that you have been a victim before you can become a Survivor. No one can be a Survivor without first having been a victim.

Now embrace yourself! You are alive!

You are not a victim for long. You will change daily. Events around us shape us into what we are today. You will have low, low valleys and moments on the peak of the mountain. It will be hard at times, so hard that you may want to find something harmful to help you cope. When that happens, find something healthy like exercise. Walk in the grass barefoot, feel the energy that the earth gives you. Start a journal, or draw, even if you think (or have been told) that you are not good at it. Art is in the eye of the beholder, always remember that.

I like to journal because I can say exactly in one word, a picture, or a thousand words how I feel, or things I am thinking about that I would not want to speak aloud. If you don't know how, start with one word, picture, or phrase. Splash all around the page in whatever direction you want and allow anything, no matter what, to come up to your mind. That is healing, that is letting go. That is healthy.

I did not know for years why I did not place value on myself. Find your value. You may not understand what I am saying, and it's hard to put into words, but think on it. Make a list of your "good things" you like about yourself, no matter how small they may seem.

One major thing for me was accepting that sexual assault is a big deal and there is no "overreaction." You cannot overreact. Never let anyone tell you to "just get over it and let it go." Many people say that, but that is because they are not knowledgeable about rape. Don't shove your feelings away and try to ignore them, or you will end up with a Pandora's Box of burdens you cannot carry. Deal with your feelings! Face them! Embrace them, even, and own them! They are yours! They are not wrong! There's no "normal" when it comes to sexual assault and how we cope, because rape is not normal. There is only "common." Throw away the word "normal" and use "common."

When you can, do research on the characteristics of people who rape. This will help you answer the question, "Why do they do it?" Do a lot of reading because knowledge is power. Knowledge is free, knowledge is healing.

You will have moments when something you did before was okay but now scares you or makes you uncomfortable. These are triggers, and are very common. Write them down. Write down your dreams and nightmares the very minute you wake up, in as much detail as you can. There are clues to understanding that are often in those details. Your brain is trying to make sense of things, so work with it. Don't just try to forget, because you will never truly be able to. Accept and grow from it.

As I am writing this letter I realize how many of these things I wish someone had told me. They would have saved me much heartache and given me hope for recovery and healing. If you remember nothing else, remember that you are not alone. Always, always, always remember that.

If you talk, it helps. You may not know what to say at first, but in time it will come. Speaking out takes back your power, your control. Crying is also okay. If you want to cry, cry. If you need to scream, scream! I have done both and afterward I was so tired…not only emotionally, but physically. But I felt better. Do not hold back! If you don't want anyone to know you are crying, cry in the shower. Let that, not rape, be your secret to keep.

Do not give up. You can make it. You will make it, whatever that means to you, as long as your steps are healthy. So be good to yourself, love yourself, stand up, don't give up, and don't give in. Those who hurt you do not have you, or who you can become.

Accept that they stole something. Acknowledge it and then that you still have your life! You have a life that can continue to grow. You have a life that can be full of simple pleasures, even as simple as watching it rain and feeling the earth grow and brighten. Find your simple moments and make them huge.

Always, always, always remember that you are not alone. Take these positive thoughts and energies from me, and accept that family that you have become a part of. You are a Survivor! You are alive! Embrace life! Happiness is yours to take.

Love,
Your sister ,Kiera Samantha

There is no formula to have a need to rea[d] [this] letter. You could be female, male, young, o[ld]... matter. You may have been victimized once... [l]ife could hold multiple accounts of pain... [b]e seeking these words as a fresh victim, [or one] who has suffered for many years and neve[r]... peace. Whatever your story may be, if you... [fo]und this letter, it is written for you.

Though Survivors are all connected by... strength, compassion, and perseverance, all... [w]e unique as well. Please know that you... [b]oth amazing and disappointing people on... [ju]st as you do in every other one of life's... [Y]ou may find that people don't believe you... use your story against you, or even those... and ignore what you told them. Even... [di]sappointing people cause you more pain,... [d]o not give up! You are worth this!... [w]e all are. The journey through healing fr... [i]s scary, painful, frustrating, depressing, and... [o]f all, the most important and rewarding jour... will ever make!

I am a Survivor of multiple rapes. I find... [of rape] therapy focus' on one rape at a ti... [nu]mber of accounts was so many that...

Dear Survivor,

There is no formula to have a need to read this letter. You could be female, male, young, old, it doesn't matter. You may have been victimized once or your life could hold multiple accounts of pain. You may be seeking these words as a recent victim or as one who has suffered for many years and never found peace. Whatever your story may be, if you have found this letter, it is written for you.

Though Survivors are all connected by our strength, compassion, and perseverance, all of us are unique as well. Please know that you will meet both amazing and disappointing people on this journey, just as you do in every other one of life's journeys. You may find people that don't believe you, betray you, use your story against you, or even those that discount and ignore what you told them. Even when others cause you more pain, please do not give up! You are worth this! Why? Because we all are. The journey through healing from rape is scary, painful, frustrating, depressing, but also the most important and rewarding journey you will ever make!

I am a Survivor of multiple rapes. My number of accounts was so many that I couldn't recall all of them. It was so frustrating, and some therapists didn't know what to do with me because I didn't fit their mold. But I was not crazy at all, I was human. A human's mind can only hold so much.

...inally, and most painful for m...
family to turn to. My biological fo...
family at all. They blamed me for...
abusive, and neglected even my m...
This made my journey much more...
...id not make it impossible. Even...
...ot be able to see it right now,). you...
...es in your life. To say it in the wo...
...a friends, "The bond that links yo...
...f blood, but of respect and...
...I do members of one fa...
...what that means...
...al family reacts...
...ES NOT seal you...
...he it. Please under...

...u cannot sit around and wait to...
...ust chase it with all you have.
...omeone you trust. If they do not res...
...makes you feel like a weight ho...
...chest, or if they make you feel...
... else. Surround yourself with p...
...nd encourage you. This will he...
...s be easier to bear. When those...
...ame, it helped me to make da...
...n if it was just to get up, taki...
...was a day. I was worth doing...
...nd of the choices that had to...
...o, success does not mean finish...
...s no such thing as completin...
...either has any other Surviv...
...s gives me more credibilit...

You do not have to remember every moment of every account in order to heal. I still have blanks too. Each aspect of someone's story brings a different layer to the puzzle and this is not an exception.

I am also a Survivor of attempted murder. This has by far been the most difficult thing in my healing. Because of my situation at the time of my rapes, I had come to truly believe that I was going to die and there was nothing I could do about it. To process this took a lot of hard work! None of this happened overnight. I still struggle with this point, so you are not alone in this. I can't stress that point enough because during my early stages of healing I felt incredibly alone and isolated.

Finally, and most painful for me, I never had a family to turn to. My biological family was not a family at all. They blamed me for being raped, were abusive, and neglected even my most basic of needs. This made my journey much more difficult, but did not make it impossible. Even though you may not be able to see it right now, you are loved deeply by others in your life. To say it in the words of one of my dear friends, "The bond that links your true family is not blood,

...ease talk to someone you trust. It
... way that makes you feel like a...
lifted off your chest, or if they mak...
talk to someone else. Surround yourse... with
love, support, and encourage you. This will...
...ugh moments be easier to bear. When th...
...oments do come, it helped me to make...
...myself. Even if it was just to get up, t...
and eat three meals a day. I was worth doing... for
myself. It was one of the choices that had to be mad...
to succeed. Also, success does not mean finishing this
journey. There is no such thing as completing this. I
have not and neither has any other Survivor. Not havin...
"completed" this gives me more credibility. Since each
person creates a new self on this journey, there is no
"normal" to work towards. Just work on you.
And, finally, when you are sitting, thinking, and feeling
truly alone, know that I, along with millions of other
survivors, are supporting you, standing behind you, and
comforting you.

"Someone chose to make me a victim, but it is
I that day did to become a Survivor."

With love always,
Stephanie
Your Fellow Survivor

but of respect and joy in each other's lives. Rarely do members of one family grow up under the same roof." That means that how your biological family reacts to your rape DOES NOT seal your fate on whether or not you will make it. Although having a good family helps in this journey, whether you make it or not is up to YOU and your choices.

Remember that regardless of what happened to you, you do deserve to heal. You deserve to love and be loved. You deserve to laugh, to cry, to do your favorite hobbies, to go to your favorite places, and to follow whatever path you choose. You are so worth it! The people that fail at this journey (and there are many who do), fail because they do not choose to take these steps. You cannot sit around and wait for healing, you must chase it with all you have.

Talk to someone you trust. If they do not respond in a way that makes you feel like a weight has been lifted off your chest, or if they make you feel worse, talk to someone else. Surround yourself with people that love, support, and encourage you. This will help the tough moments become easier to bear. When those tough moments do come it helps me to make daily goals for myself, even if it was just to get up, take a shower, and eat three meals that day. I was worth doing that for myself. It was one of the choices that had to be made for me to succeed.

Also, success does not mean finishing this journey. There is no such thing as completing this; I have not, and neither has any other Survivor. Acknowledging I have not "completed" this journey gives me more credibility. Since each person creates a new self on their journey, there is no "normal" to work towards. Just work on you.

And, finally, when you are sitting, thinking, and feeling truly alone, know that I, along with millions of other Survivors, are supporting you, standing behind you, and comforting you.

"Someone chose to make me a victim, but it is I who decided to become a Survivor."

With love always, Stephanie
Your Fellow Survivor

Don't allow fear to make your choices for you. Every time you catch yourself shying from something you want to do because you believe being a victim prevents it, call yourself on it.

Each Survivor's transformation happens in its own way. But every hopeful step, every healthy action you do, every time you become better than you were yesterday, you are defying your betrayers. Every glimpse of positive transformation is your victory and your betrayers' defeat.

How do you know when you have become a Survivor? It's when you are no longer ashamed to be a Survivor.

Survivor-

Where to start? I can only offer you
experience, although all of our stories
unique. The one thing we share is
we are survivors and we will all
it through this mess of a journey
d rape. I know I am different in hou.
andle my trauma - I am extroverted ar.s'
activist. It's the only way I know
w to heal. Where others will offer
ou hugs and unconditional love, I
ill offer you strength and confidence.
at's all I know. Together, as a grou
survivors will make it

Dear Survivor,

Where to start? I can only offer you my experience, although all of our stories are unique. The one thing we share is that we are Survivors and we will all make it through this mess of a journey called rape. I know I am different in how I handle my trauma — I am extroverted and an activist. It's the only way I know how to heal. Where others will offer you hugs and unconditional love, I will offer you strength and confidence. That's all I know. Together, as a group, we Survivors will make it.

I reported my most recent rape. I didn't report the ones in the past out of embarrassment and fear. This one was different. I was scared for my life. I thought reporting was the right thing to do. My friends told me it was the right thing to do. Since then, I have faced such retribution and judgment. I had to move, I've lost money, I've lost friends, I've given up many things that are important to me…I've even lost parts of myself. I have doubted my conviction that reporting my rapist was the best choice. He has been sitting in jail for 8 months awaiting trial…but I have been on trial in public judgment. There were times that I wanted to kill myself or run away where no one knows me. And other times I've wondered how I could raise my daughter in this horrible world.

...before day one of my trial...

...ing. I know it's good I will have the chance to be heard...

...But nobody told my how scared I'd...

...would be. So, was it the right thing to...

wrong... those words shouldn't even factor in to...

It's completely personal. If you decide to report, know that you are not alone. You may feel alone and lost in the system, but many survivors have been there and we'll be there. Please don't be afraid to reach out. And, if you don't report, boy do I understand! I have lost count of how many times I wished I had let this go. At the same time, I do enjoy the thought of my rapist, wearing his orange jumpsuit, orange socks, orange shoes (I saw him in pretrial so I will forever have the orange image burned in my head) rotting in a jail cell. He's waiting there for trial wh... the words and conviction of a survivor will put him in prison where he belongs. In the end, I think I'm glad I reported. At least he can't hurt me or anyone else again. And, I stood up for myself... after all h... threats and abuse. Me. A survivor.

I'm so sorry you had to go through this. No one deserves it. Please find someone to talk to. And always, always know that you are

And now, two weeks before day one of my trial, I am shaking. I know it's good I will have the chance to be heard in court. But nobody told me how scary this whole process would be. So, was it the right thing to do? Right, wrong…those words shouldn't even factor in here. It's completely personal. If you decide to report, know that you are not alone. You may feel alone and lost in the system, but many Survivors have been there and will be there. Please don't be afraid to reach out. And if you don't report, boy do I understand! I have lost count of how many times I wished I had let this go. At the same time, I do enjoy the thought of my rapist, wearing his orange jumpsuit, orange socks, orange shoes (I saw him in pretrial so I will forever have the orange image burned in my head), rotting in a jail cell. He's waiting there for a trial where the words and conviction of a Survivor will put him in prison where he belongs. In the end, I think I'm glad I reported. At least he can't hurt me or anyone else again. And, I stood up for myself…after all his threats and abuse. Me. A Survivor.

I'm so sorry you had to go through this. No one deserves it. Please find someone to talk to. And always, always know that you are not at fault. The only person that can cause rape is a rapist. Let's join together and spread the word about how we survive – stronger and better than ever!

We can do it!

Love, Joanna

♡ Joanna

P.S. It's been 2 weeks since I wrote this. Tomorrow I go to trial to kick some Rapist ass!!

Joanna mailed this letter directly from the District Attorney's office. Two days later, she won her case in court.

In 2007, a man abducted a five-year-old girl from her yard in Oklahoma and raped her. He was apprehended and in 2010 was sentenced to six consecutive life terms plus 41 years.

This is the statement that the girl, known only as the "Broken Arrow Angel," made directly to her rapist in court...at age 8.

You need to respect your punishment. That was a bad thing you did. I don't want you hurting anybody else. That is why you should be in jail forever, so accept it. God made you, but you are not like God's person. You are the devil's person. You should have been on God's side and this would never happen. Back then I was a little angel fish and you were a great white shark. Now I am the great white shark and you are the little clown fish. I'm going to forget all about you and go on with my life, and how I want it to be without any bad person stopping me. I was only five years old, now I am eight.

I'm going to be what God wants me to be,

and nothing's stopping me.

Especially you.

Matt Atkinson is a Domestic and Sexual Violence Response Professional. He has worked as a director of prevention of domestic and sexual violence, where he developed and implemented programs with women's prisons, university sports teams, churches, schools, and Indian tribes. Matt has also counseled youth and adults, including more than 500 Survivors of rape.

In 2004, he became the first male given the *National Award for Outstanding Advocacy and Community Work in Ending Sexual Violence* by the National Sexual Violence Resource Center. In 2005 he was awarded "Most Therapeutic" by his colleagues. In 2006 he began to teach university courses on domestic violence and crisis intervention. In 2010, he wrote *You Can Take Your Power Back: A Guide To Your Rights After Rape*, which has been distributed to thousands of victims. He is regularly sought as a presenter/trainer at workshops and conferences.

Matt is currently directing a project to implement new Sexual Assault Response Teams to serve victims of sexual violence, and he runs an annual Spiritual Healing Retreat for Survivors which draws participants from around the world (see www.resurrectionafterrape.org for info).

Matt has two Bachelor's and a Master's Degree in Art/ Human Physiology, Behavioral Science, and Social Work. He is very happily married to the most amazing woman in the world, and has two incredible sons. Matt is an Ojibway *Oshkaabewis* (pipe-keeper) and regularly participates in ceremonies.

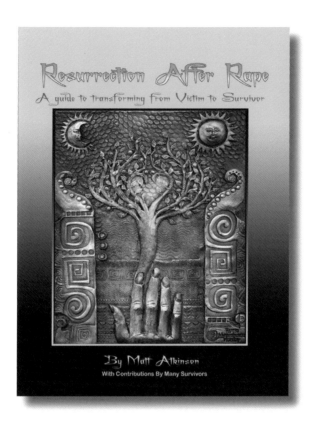

Also Available:
Resurrection After Rape:
A Guide to Transforming from Victim to Survivor

Critically acclaimed as an instant classic in the science of rape recovery, *Resurrection After Rape* is used as a textbook in college courses, and is the primary guidebook in many counseling centers and rape crisis programs for treating rape trauma in therapy.

Available at **www.resurrectionafterrape.org**, Amazon.com, and barnesandnoble.com

Visit **www.letterstosurvivors.com** for more resources, to join a web community of Survivors, and to learn about bonus *Letters To Survivors* materials.

CPSIA information can be obtained at www.ICGtesting.com
Printed in the USA
BVIW12n1455250115
384869BV00001B/3

* 9 7 8 1 4 5 0 7 2 8 8 3 6 *